OPTIMAL D FILTER USING ARTIFICIAL INTELLIGENCE TECHNIQUES

BY

MANIDIPA NAT

OPTIMAL DESIGN OF WAVEGUIDE FILTER USING ARTIFICIAL INTELLIGENCE TECHNIQUES

BY

MANIDIPA NATH

CONTENTS

List of Contents   **Page No.**

LIST OF FIGURES

Figure No.   **Page No.**

viii

LIST OF TABLES

ACRONYMS

ADS	Agilent's Advanced Design System
AI	Artificial Intelligence
AMC	Artificial Magnetic Conductor
ANN	Artificial Neural Networks
BP	Band Pass
BPF	Band Pass Filter
BSF	Band Stop Filter
BW	Bandwidth
CAD	Computer Aided Design
CEM	Computational Electro-Magnetic
CFBEM	Finite and Boundary Element Methods
CST	Computer Simulation Technology
CPU	Central Processing Unit
DC	Direct Current
EBG	Electromagnetic Band Gap
FBW	Fractional Band-Width
EM	Electro Magnetic
FDFD	Finite Difference Frequency Domain
FDTD	Finite Difference Time Domain
FE	Finite Element
FEM	Finite Element Method
FIT	Finite Integral Technique
FSS	Frequency Selective Surfaces
GA	Genetic Algorithm
GAM	Generalized Admittance Matrix
GSM	Generalized Scattering Matrix
HFSS	High Frequency Structure Simulator
HP	High Pass
HPF	High Pass Filter
HTS	High Temperature Superconductor
LP	Low Pass
LPF	Low Pass Filter
MATLAB	Matrix Laboratory
MEMS	Micro-Electro-Mechanical Systems

MMIC	Monolithic Microwave Integrated Circuit
MOM	Method of Moments
NN	Neural Network
1D	One dimensional
PBC/PML	Periodic Boundary Condition /
	Perfectly Matched Layer
PBG	Photonic Band Gap
PCB	Printed Circuit Board
PEC	Perfect Electric Conductor
PMC	Perfect Magnetic Conductor
PSO	Particle Swarm Optimization
Q	Quality factor
RF	Radio Frequency
SA	Simulated Annealing
SMA	Subminiature Version A
SSL	Suspended Strip Line
TE	Transverse Electric
TEM	Transverse-Electromagnetic
TLM	Transmission Line Method
TM	Transverse Magnetic
2D	Two Dimensional
3 D	Three Dimensional
UAV	Unmanned Air Vehicles
UWB	Ultra Wide Band
VNA	Vector network analyzers

1

INTRODUCTION AND LITERATURE SURVEY

1.1 INTRODUCTION

In this chapter a brief review on filters, types, design techniques and applications are discussed. In addition fundamental concept of electromagnetic (EM) wave propagation inside waveguide, its utility and applications, optimal band-pass filter (BPF) design using Artificial Intelligence (AI) techniques, simulation, fabrication and measurement techniques of waveguide based filters are discussed in brief. Motivation, scope of the research work done so far and organization of this thesis has been included in this chapter. The research work carried out so far on the chosen topic and a clear picture of the achievements done so far to complete the thesis has been included briefly in this chapter and elaborated in respective chapters of this thesis.

1.1.1 REVIEW OF FILTERS

Filters are very important component in the microwave and Radio Frequency (RF) communication systems. A filter is a device that produces a prescribed response for a given excitation and is designed to transmit Electro-Magnetic (EM) frequencies in certain pass-band region and rejects undesirable signal frequencies outside the pass-band with high attenuation in those regions. The fundamental use of filters in electrical engineering is to shape signal spectrum and to reduce noise in receivers /spurious emissions in transmitters.

A filter is characterized by one or more pass bands or one or more stop bands. Depending on the frequency response characteristics filters are categorized into four main types i) Low Pass Filter (LPF),ii) High Pass Filter (HPF),iii) Band Pass Filter (BPF),iv) Band Stop Filter (BSF). The frequency response of a filter is defined in terms of location of the poles and zeros of transfer function. Microwave filters have traditionally been built using different structures of waveguide, printed circuits and coaxial lines. Design and analysis tools for such filters are based on EM field theory. EM simulation tools are generally used for accurate prediction of the filter response and can also be used to optimize its performance. In recent years, filters with stringent requirements are necessary in many applications of RF/microwave and extensive research work using new technologies has already been published /reported in literature [1-3].

1

Desired parameters that decide filter performance are called specifications. Modern filters having critical specifications are required for applications where RF, microwave and millimeter-wave frequency ranges are concerned. The major application areas are in defense, space, communication systems, commercial sectors, wireless communication and its expansion into cost effective applications for radar, security, medical field etc.

Microwave and Millimeter wave frequencies are used for advanced communication systems for wireless applications where wide BW and compact high performance filters are required for specific applications in Microwave Integrated Circuits (MIC), Monolithic Microwave Integrated Circuit (MMIC), Micro-Electro-Mechanical Systems (MEMS) and planar antennas.

Various structures available for waveguide based filters are SIW, CPW, Ridge waveguide, Fin line, E plane, H plane, Inter-digital, Comb-line etc. Printed circuit filters are based on different configurations as microstrip, stripline, suspended substrate and its variations. Stepped-impedance, ladder line, pseudo inter-digital line, hairpin resonator, multilayer, coupled-line are most commonly used forms of printed filters.

1.1.2 FILTER AS A RESEARCH TOPIC

The frequency response characteristics of filters are nonlinear but can be predicted using a finite number of polynomial terms depending on the amplitude characteristics of the filter. These properties are ideally suitable for Artificial Neural Network (ANN) modeling. Filters designed for RF/microwave applications generally has stringent requirement of frequency response along with physical specifications of smaller size, lighter weight and lower cost [4-6]. Advances in Computer Aided Design (CAD) tools such as full-wave EM simulators have revolutionized filter design [7]. However, availability of manpower and expertise is essential to use EM simulation tools. Otherwise lack of experience generally leads toward cut and try design and makes wastage of time and resources. Hence fitness provides excellent research opportunity, particularly with respect to usage of soft computing paradigms.

1.2 MOTIVATION OF WORK

Filters were chosen as research topic as some knowledge /skill gained from previous experience has been used to work further and Band Pass Filter (BPF) configuration is chosen here for the purpose of research on filters. It has been studied that Artificial Intelligence (AI) based techniques are less resource oriented and used for fast modeling and optimization of systems suitable for various design applications. In many institutions where costly software tools are not available these design techniques can be adopted for optimal design of parameters of any device within a certain frequency band. So this motivated the author to do fundamental research on optimization of BW of microwave filters using AI techniques. However, as per available literature the computing approach has been applied only to a limited extent so far. The motivation and goal of this work is to extend the same as far as possible.

1.2.1 SCOPE OF WORK

Application of AI techniques for performance enhancement of the filter structure under consideration and optimal design of filters are main area under the scope of work where emphasis has been made. The range of design parameters are required to be determined for development of optimal filter. Further fabrication and measurement steps can be taken to assess the optimal filter [8-9] quantitatively.

Artificial Neural Network (ANN) model of filters are useful in optimization problems and this technique of modeling filters has great potential. Here scope of the present work is

(i)   A suitable alternative process to solve optimization problems is to use AI techniques. The trained ANN model can be used with different soft computing techniques to compute the optimal solution.ANN technique along with suitable optimization algorithm can be utilized to compute optimal frequency responses of filters for applications where optimal responses are required within a short time which may not be achievable using EM simulation.

(ii) The frequency response of a filter can be obtained from its trained and tested ANN model for a particular frequency band of interest. Some parameters of the trained ANN model can be further optimized using Genetic Algorithm (GA) / Particle Swarm Optimization (PSO) algorithm within a particular frequency band.

1.2.1.1 OPTIMAL DESIGN OF FILTERS USING ARTIFICIAL INTELLIGENCE (AI)

ANN, GA and PSO algorithms are used in this thesis for the synthesis/design/optimization of one waveguide filter and two different planar filters. Specifically the works carried out in this thesis are listed below.

(i)   Application of ANN and GA techniques for design of optimal filter using **Rectangular Waveguide BPF at X band** where design and optimization are carried out on a rectangular waveguide structure having multiple dielectric posts. It has been observed that design parameters of the rectangular waveguide having multiple posts can be selected to perform as filter in microwave frequency range. In addition to that the structure can be optimized for broad filter BW using ANN and GA technique. Trained ANN model of filter structure having multiple vertical cylindrical dielectric posts inside a rectangular waveguide can be used to predict scattering (S) properties of the same within reasonable accuracy. The training/testing data of S parameters can be generated from semi analytical technique of computation based on image theory and further utilized to develop the trained/tested ANN model of the filter for a particular frequency band. GA can be used to optimize the frequency response of S parameters of the

3

filter within the frequency band under consideration. Optimized response of filters using configuration other than multi-post waveguide can also be obtained using AI techniques.

(ii)   Here **Suspended Strip-Line (SSL) BPF for K to Ka band** is considered and has been optimized using ANN/GA techniques. The computed frequency response of the optimal filter was compared with that of the measured response to verify the suitability of selected AI techniques for design of optimal filter under consideration.

(ii)   Application of ANN and PSO for optimal filter development where design, optimization and performance verifications is carried out on **Microstrip ring BPF for S-C band**. Here microstrip based ring filter configuration has been optimized using ANN/PSO techniques and computed frequency responses of optimal ring filter is compared with that of the measured response. The basic aim of this research is to establish the suitability of optimization techniques under consideration in place of EM simulation using BPF having multiple ring configuration realized with microstrip line.

1.3 LITERATURE SURVEY

Here extensive survey has been made on recent literature regarding waveguide and EM mode propagation inside the guide for microwave frequency ranges. Analysis of S parameters of a structure having inductive obstacles and working as discontinuity inside a waveguide has already been investigated by pioneer researchers. Theoretically analyses to compute scattering parameters of the structure under consideration are useful for utilization of the same as BPF. Here separate sections containing the prerequisite of the research work on optimal design of BPF using different structures are included. The literature survey for previous works on optimization of BW of BPF has been done and presented in this chapter.

1.3.1 FUNDAMENTALS OF WAVEGUIDES

A waveguide is a microwave transmission line [10-11] that uses only a single conductor and can be used to guide EM energy. A typical rectangular waveguide structure shown in Figure 1.1 has low attenuation and excellent power-handling capability suitable for design of filters. It is usable to frequencies in excess of 1.0 GHz and can provide precision that is not ordinarily available in coaxial lines or strip transmission lines. Transmission line operates from zero to some high frequency and is inefficient in microwave frequency ranges due to skin effect and dielectric losses. Waveguide can be operated in a certain frequency range between cutoff and second higher order modal frequency.

Waveguide can be realized in a medium where wave motion can be characterized by the One Dimensional (1D) wave equation [12-14]. The traveling waves propagate unchanged as long as the wave impedance of the medium is constant. When the wave impedance changes, signal scattering occurs, i.e. a traveling wave impinging on an impedance discontinuity will partially reflect and partially transmit at the junction in such a way that energy is conserved.

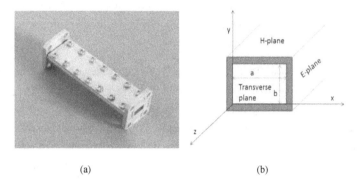

(a)   (b)

Figure 1.1 Structure of rectangular waveguide (a) filter (b) transmission line configuration

Figure 1.2 Different structures of rectangular waveguide filter

Waveguide has a number of advantages over coax, micro-strip and strip-line. Being completely shielded it can transmit extremely high peak powers and has very low loss at microwave frequencies. Disadvantage of waveguides are its high cost, low manufacturing volumes, expensive materials (copper and silver) for construction. Because waveguide uses a single conductor, it cannot provide a Transverse-Electro-Magnetic (TEM) mode of transmission. The desired modes used in waveguide have distinct lowest cutoff frequencies.

Electric /Magnetic fields that exist inside a waveguide must obey Maxwell's field equations. In order to satisfy the boundary conditions imposed by the walls of the guides, there can be no tangential component of electric field at walls of the waveguide if the walls are perfect conductor. According to Maxwell's equations, EM waves do not pass through conductors, they are reflected by conductors. Electric field lines that touch a conductor must be perpendicular to it. Magnetic field lines close to a conductor must be parallel to it. There are, therefore, different field orientations that meet these requirements, accordingly each such orientation is referred to as mode and only certain modes of propagation carries flow of power generated inside waveguide.

A rectangular waveguide supports Transverse Electric (TE) and Transverse Magnetic (TM) waves and is used in many applications including millimeter wave and high power systems. The dominant mode is TE_{10} and is the desired one that propagates in the waveguide. The TE_{10} mode is the normal mode in which energy propagates inside rectangular waveguide. In this case, none of the electric field lines cross the transverse plane, they always remain within the E-plane and are normal to the broad wall of the waveguide. In TE_{01} mode magnetic field lines are circular in the H-plane and are normal to the short wall. The maximum positive and negative electric field crests of the wave travel down the center of the waveguide along the broad dimension and the electric field decreases to zero along the waveguide's narrow side walls.

Rectangular, circular, elliptical and in general all hollow, metallic waveguides cannot support TEM waves. In the X-band rectangular waveguide, only TE_{10} mode (dominant mode of the waveguide) can propagate within 6.56 GHz $\leq$ f $\leq$ 13.12 GHz. Wave guide filters can be of rectangular, circular, coaxial or dielectric resonator type. Few BPF structures based on rectangular waveguide are shown in Figure 1.2. Conventional techniques for design of waveguide BPF are available in standard literature [4-6].

1.3.1.1 UTILITY OF WAVEGUIDE IN MICROWAVE APPLICATIONS

Waveguide components operate over a very wide frequency band and with a wide range of functions. Frequency bands associated with waveguide range from 0.32 GHz to 110 GHz and components include Filters, Circulators, Directional-couplers, Power-dividers, Diplexers, Multiplexers, Mixers, Isolators, Amplifiers, Attenuators and Loads. These components can be designed using specialized synthesis techniques, of which simulation is an integral part.

Microwave and millimeter-wave components for wireless communication systems and radars are traditionally built with waveguide technology that offers low-loss and high Quality factor (Q). Waveguide filters are useful at higher frequencies and widely used in high power applications because of their low-loss performance. The advantage of waveguide filters over the planar structure is Q factor (typical 500 at 30.0 GHz) and the disadvantage is the volume.

To meet increasing demand for microwave filters and antennas in wireless, terrestrial, satellite-based communications and for radar applications, accurate and efficient CAD tools are required and can be applied to microwave filter design, simulation, modeling and validation. The recent advances in CAD for RF/microwave circuits, particularly full-wave EM simulation tools are implemented using commercial and specific in-house software.

1.3.1.2 ANALYSIS OF WAVEGUIDE DISCONTINUITY

Scattered fields from obstacles inside a waveguide can be represented by superposition of propagating and evanescent modes having boundary conditions. To determine the effect of the obstacle on the propagating modes inside the waveguide, the structure as shown in Figure 1.3-1.4 has been considered here. A set of reference planes far enough from the obstacle has been chosen where all the evanescent fields have decayed to negligible amplitude and the obstacle can be characterized entirely by the amplitudes of the propagating modes. Far from the obstacle, only propagating modes are present and the dominant mode is allowed to propagate. In this condition the region within the reference planes are characterized by two complex numbers, the reflection coefficient and the transmission coefficient.

A full height conducting or dielectric post inserted inside a rectangular waveguide acts as discontinuity and the effect of scattering fields from conducting and dielectric posts inside rectangular waveguide has been a subject of interest to researchers for many years. The post is perpendicular to the direction of propagation or the axis of the rectangular waveguide as shown in Figure 1.3. Figure 1.4 shows Two-Dimensional (2D) view of rectangular waveguide structure having single and dual dielectric post configuration. Three-Dimensional (3D) view of cylindrical dielectric posts in multi layer configurations with uniform radius and spacing inside rectangular waveguide is shown in Figure 1.5.

Marcuvitz [10] calculated the parameters of the equivalent circuit for a circular dielectric post discontinuity in a rectangular waveguide. Nielsen [15] developed a theory based upon the method of expanding the field in a sum of modes which is applicable to circular centered posts but is extended to posts of any size and complex permittivity. A single-post as well as multiple-post loaded rectangular waveguide [16-17] has already been analyzed by researchers using various methods. A complete analysis of homogeneous dielectric posts of the inductive type in rectangular waveguide was developed by Leviatan and Sheaffer [18]. The post was replaced by a set of unknown current filaments placed on or inside the post surface. The analysis of the structure has been done using multifilament current model. Due to the variation of the electric-field intensity in the dielectric region thicker post with higher permittivity is desirable to produce appreciable changes of incident signal by reflection/transmission which can be measured.

Conducting posts become lossy at high frequencies and dissipates energy but dielectric posts can have lower losses and are more efficient at high microwave and millimeter wave frequencies. Scattering by dielectric posts in a rectangular waveguide was investigated using a Combination of the Finite and Boundary Element Methods (CFBEM), and the equivalent circuits derived by Kiyoshi and Koshiba [19]. The interaction between two posts and resonances formed due to lossless dielectric posts in a rectangular waveguide were realized by a lattice circuit. A configuration of arbitrarily shaped multiple dielectric posts in waveguide were analyzed by Jiang and Li [20]. The analysis was

7

based on moment methods and the combination of the finite and boundary element methods although the derivations became very complicated with increasing number of post.

Figure 1.3 3D view of (a) Single dielectric post configuration inside rectangular waveguide (b) A single-post obstacle inside a rectangular waveguide(enlarged view) [18]

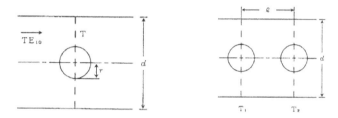

Figure 1.4 2D view of (a) Centered dielectric post in rectangular waveguide [17], (b) Rectangular waveguide loaded with two posts [17]

These concepts are useful in designing microwave filters having multiple posts inside rectangular waveguide where physical parameters of the posts can be varied according to the desired filter response of the structure [21-23]. When filters of higher Q are desired, either one large post having higher radii or a multiple-post configuration is suitable or optimization is required to compute the filter parameters for best possible response of the same. Considering design limitations and fabrication tolerances proper design methodology is required where final simulation/measurement results of the filter will not deviate significantly from the desired one. Available resources and infrastructure can be used to design /develop the filter.

1.3.2 WAVEGUIDE BAND PASS FILTER (BPF)

There are different categories of filters depending on frequency response characteristics and physical constructions. The BW of a filter are evaluated in terms of range of frequencies within which the S parameters are within a specified value. The BW is a function of coupling of resonator elements, resonator size, resonator spacing, ground plane separation and material of fabrication. Utility of a filter are primarily dependent on its pass band along with other specifications. Physical and dimensional parameters of a filter plays major role in deciding frequency response and utility of the same over a specific frequency band. User defined specifications of any filter is required to study for its feasibility and expertise of a person is required to decide correct filter topology for specific applications.

In the domain of research it is not possible to concentrate on all categories of filter. So here a particular type of filter is chosen where a new procedure is adopted to implement design and optimization methods for development of the filter using existing technologies. Generally BPFs are choosen in most of the communication applications (mobile, satellite, terristrial). The main focus of this thesis work is to design and optimize filters having BP response using AI techniques and to replace use of EM simulator for predicting the characteristics of the same. Recent literature survey reflects that few reported results on the chosen topic are available for reference [9] for this research work and it has been observed that there are scopes to do fundamental research to design/optimize BPF configurations using AI techniques in place of EM simulation tools.

The filter topologies and configurations are required to be chosen according to its applications. Optimal design of filters under consideration can be done using soft computing techniques. EM simulation tools are generally used to compute frequency response of S parameters of any filter structure. With the advances in analysis methods like mode matching method, finite integral techniques, finite element methods and full wave EM simulation techniques, frequency responses of waveguide filters can be predicted accurately. Either hand written code or commercially available software based on these techniques is useful for analysis and characterization of the waveguide based filters.

Design and synthesis of waveguide filters can be done (i) using theoretical expressions for reflectance and transmittance of the same by solving Maxwell equation in frequency domain and by using appropriate basis function for the filter structure under consideration. The frequency dependent characteristics of the BPF configuration based on waveguide structure can be computed using software codes and compared with the characteristics required to achieve. The process of iterative design cycle (optimization) may continue until theoretically computed frequency response of the filter reaches the desired value within reasonable accuracy. The optimal design of the BPF can be used for practical fabrication of the same.

1.3.2.1 APPLICATIONS OF WAVEGUIDE BPF

Waveguide BPF performs valuable functions in microwave equipment used in satellite communications, electronic warfare, radar, automatic test equipment and various microwave multiplexers. Precise performance of waveguide filters are required for application like satellite communication, terrestrial systems, diplexing circuit of the feed systems of the satellite-borne or ground station antennas where waveguide filters having narrow bandwidth, low loss, smaller size and higher power handling capacity are used [24]. Microwave filters used for space communication systems are traditionally implemented with waveguide technology, mainly due to low losses and high power handling capability issues. Waveguide filter configurations as shown in Figure 1.6 are based on SSL, metal-insert, inter-digital [25-26, 40-42,73-83] and generally used for frequencies higher than 20.0 GHz.

Broadband filters have applications [43-64] depending on its structure and frequency responses and are not suitable for satellite based specific applications; Literature studies [24-63] show that waveguide structures are not preferable for broadband filter applications compared to other transmission line structures.

The E-plane waveguide BPF and the iris-coupled waveguide BPF have good manufacturability, improved stop band performance and reduced physical size [40-45]. Practically E plane rectangular waveguide filters are not suitable for space applications. Waveguide filters are widely used in microwave systems and communication module of satellite transponders due to their very low insertion loss. In space communication system microwave waveguide filter having narrow bandwidth (0.2%-2%) are required for satellite payload [24, 28-31]. A satellite communication system uses waveguide filter having moderate bandwidth up-to 10% in its payload [32-35].Depending on specific service provided by each payload, filters used in satellite communication system can cover a wide range of frequencies (spectral band ranging from 100 MHz - 40 GHz.).

For narrow bandwidth applications waveguide filters are suitable for use in satellite communication in the terrestrial part. Waveguide dual-mode pseudo-elliptic filter are often used in satellite applications due to its high Q, compact size and sharp selectivity [31]. It has been studied that BP and BS filters can be designed and optimized using rectangular waveguide having multiple dielectric posts symmetrically placed inside the structure. It is observed that reasonably low loss filter response with reflection and transmission bandwidth (BW) of (1.0-10.0)% has been achieved as reported in the literature [36-38].A broadband wireless communication system, operating in microwave and millimeter wave frequencies requires wideband BPFs.

BPF using metal waveguide is used in many types of communication system but their large size, weight and manufacturing cost limit their ability to meet the demanding requirements of many present day filter applications. Unmanned Air Vehicles (UAV), satellite communications and phased array antennas are most desirable applications of filters.

Available literature [36-45] indicates that application of waveguide based filters at X-band is not for satellite application and space communication applications. Recent literatures study shows very little information on broadband waveguide filters having transmittance more than 20.0% and hence it is not possible to include applications of broadband waveguide filters for satellite based systems in the reference list. Fabrication techniques of waveguide BPF is available in standard text books and literature [114-115].

Table 1.1 Reference list of different types of BPF and BW achieved

Filter Technology	Configuration	BW obtained/proposed	Reference
Rectangular Waveguide	Wideband, E plane	9.5% at 105.0 GHz 5.5 at 36.90 GHz, 2.13 at 94.0 GHz,	24-25, 43-45
	Narrow band	(0.2- 10)% upto 15 GHz.	28-31
	Inductive(H plane)	2.5% at 26 GHz, 2.265%,at 34GHz, (2-20)% at 18-40 GHz.	27
	Metal insert (E plane)	5.3% at 14.0 GHz.	26,40-42
	Dielectric post	5.0% at 9.0GHz.	36-38
	Capacitive Iris	(16-17)% at 9.25 GHz.	39
SIW	Cavity resonator	20% at 10.0,32.5% at 35.0 GHz.	32-35
Tunable coupled stub resonator	Planar broadband	76% upto 10.0 GHz.	46-48
Combline/ Interdigital	Wideband	(45-60)% upto 20 GHz.	49-51
Coupled ring resonator	Compact / wideband	(50-90)% at 2.0 GHz.	52-53
Ridge waveguide	Evanescent mode	12% 10 GHz,32.7% at 35.0,50.0% at 15.5	54-57
CPW	Compact /broadband	66% at 9.0 GHz.,110% at 6.8 GHz.	58-72
SSL	Compact/Wideband	110.0% at 6.8 GHz.	73-85
UWB	Planar ultra wideband	(70-120) % at 6.8 GHz.	86-113

1.3.3 PRINTED CIRCUIT FILTER

BPF filters designed using waveguide or coaxial lines are generally large in size. At ultra-high frequencies strip lines provide a practical means of realizing lightweight filters having compact size. Printed circuit filters have advantages over rectangular or coaxial waveguide filters in terms of low cost, repeatability and ease of integration with active circuits [116-120]. Filters using printed circuits have high insertion loss due to conductor and dielectric losses. In general BPF using printed circuit is not suitable for applications where high power and very low loss are required. Low cost, miniature filter configuration having specified pass band are generally implemented using printed circuits instead of waveguide technology. Filters having broad bandwidth are easy to implement using printed circuits like Suspended Strip Line (SSL) and microstrip where fabrication complexities are less compared to that of waveguide [121-123].

1.3.4 Techniques Available for Design and Optimization of Filter

Techniques of theoretical design, synthesis steps, analysis process and different optimization prcesses useful to meet the optimal design of a filter are avaiable in open literature [124-135]. Analytical techniques to predict electromagnetic behavior includes (i) asymptotic analysis (ii) variation analysis, (iii) integral transform, (iv) contour integration and (v) perturbation theory. Improvements in computer speed and memory helped to develop some analytical methods as Computational Electro-Magnetic (CEM) methods, Finite Element (FE) method, Finite Difference Time Domains (FDTD) and Finite Difference Frequency Domains (FDFD) methods, Transmission line matrix (TLM) method and Method of Moments (MOM) are examples of these.

Ansoft HFSS, commercial software tools [136] based on the finite element method (FEM) is used in this thesis to simulate filters based on waveguide. A complete set of simulated results (150 frequency points at X band) can be obtained in 2.6 min on a standard PC (Pentium IV at 3 GHz with 1GB RAM). A general optimization process requires the repeated use of the simulation tools and resources to support the software using PC having reasonable good configuration. The accuracy of the results are also dependent on the capability of the user to run the software efficiently using appropriate options to model the filter structure under considerations.

The design, development and optimization process of any filter involves

i) Analysis of filter configuration in terms of S parameters

   (Electrical, mechanical, environmental, and cost)

ii) Selection of an appropriate filter structure/topology

iii) Computation of filter-coupling and resonator dimensions

v) Optimization of required parameters

vi) Determination of applicable filter fabrication methods.

vii) Fabrication of prototype filter

viii) Assembly, alignment, and testing of prototype filter

ix) Generation of measured data/plot and modify/redesign/re-optimize (if necessary)

For design and optimization of filters, initial design is performed according to the requirements. Filter characteristics obtained from EM simulation are compared with that of theoretical design and the optimization parameters of the filter are altered in a systematic manner. The simulated performance of the filter is compared with the desired performance, and if the simulated filter response deviates from the desired result, the sequence of filter design, modification of optimization parameters are performed iteratively until the desired performance of the filter is achieved. CAD tools based on full-wave EM analysis are already developed and can be used for design of waveguide filters for narrow-band and wide-band applications of space communication systems [136-139].

1.3.4.1 DESIGN/OPTIMIZATION OF BPF USING AI TECHNIQUES

Here the research work has been pursued to establish the suitability of AI techniques for optimal design of filters and theoretical design, simulated results and measured results of different filter configurations are compared.There are many parameters of a filter irrespective of its configuration that can be optimized to establish the usefulness of the design methodology chosen for pursuing this research work. In this thesis the bandwidth (BW) of filter (VSWR BW and Band-Pass BW) has been taken as the parameter that has been optimized using AI techniques and optimal filters have been designed using three different configuration.

It is obvious that the reseach work to design optimal filters can be further extended i) where optimization technique other than those applied here can also be used for optimal design of filters , ii) Filter parameters other than 'bandwidth (BW)' can be chosen to design optimal filters and iii) Filter configurations other than those considered here can be choosen where optimization techniques can be applied.

In this thesis BPF having waveguide and printed circuit configuration are considered and emphasis has been made on selected research topics. Designs, development of BPF having three different configurations are carried out where optimization of VSWR BW and Band-Pass BW of the same for a frequency band is under consideration and optimization algorithms using AI techniques are used.

The thesis ventures to the area where soft computing algorithms like ANN/GA and Artificial ANN/PSO techniques are used for filter optimization. In this process filter parameter has been selected for optimization of BW of the same and appropriate fitness functions have been written to satisfy the requirements.

Soft computing techniques like ANN, GA and PSO are utilized here to design and optimize the frequency response of one waveguide filter and two printed filters. In order to verify the suitability and applicability of the optimization process for the particular design, characterizations of these filters are carried out and are included in this thesis. Measured frequency responses of the fabricated filters are compared with corresponding simulated/optimized responses to validate the design and optimization process within the frequency band of interest.

1.3.4.2 OPTIMIZATION OF WAVEGUIDE BPF

The main objective of this research is to investigate frequency response of multi-post multi-layer rectangular waveguide filter where AI techniques has been used and efforts has been made to replace extensive use of EM simulator for design of optimal waveguide filter. In order to acquaint the reader with the latest development of optimization techniques like ANN/GA/PSO for obtaining optimal response of waveguide based filters, elaborate discussions are made on i) Filter configurations under consideration,

ii) BW of waveguide based filter structures as reported in recent literature and

iii) Design/optimization using AI techniques.

The design techniques, simulation methods, fabrication processes of the waveguide filter under consideration are also discussed in details and the utility of the investigation for practical applications of the filter is also focused.

1.3.4.3 ARTIFICIAL NEURAL NETWORK (ANN)

ANN technique has been recognized as a fast and powerful tool to model EM device (filters) having nonlinear input output relationships and used to predict device behavior for which neither any simple mathematical model is neither available nor any analytical results. This methodology of design can handle a number of design variables with the desired accuracy. The main advantage of this design process is its fast response so that modeling time can be drastically reduced once an NN model is trained to follow the device behavior. A general ANN structure can be properly trained to model any passive device or system within a particular frequency range up-to any degree of accuracy and can be used repeatedly. In this process ANN model of any filter trained using known data can be used to compute approximate values of the required parameters of the same over a certain band of frequencies. The utility of ANN model of any passive device is that the structure can be dynamically adjusted for better representation of the system iteratively.

Microwave frequencies are widely used in satellite and ground based communication systems where filters are required to be designed according to the requirement of the system. User defined codes/commercial EM solvers have been utilized to design these filters for a long time through trial and error procedure. Use of ANN technique instead of EM solvers for design of microwave filters in RF and Microwave frequencies is preferred for few reasons,

(i)   The application of ANN modeling technique is an efficient replacement of the use of Electro Magnetic (EM) simulators for RF, microwave and millimeter wave communication circuit and systems design. The time domain and frequency domain EM simulators are considered efficient tools for accurate analysis and design of a component, circuit or antenna for which there is no simpler method of analysis available. RF and microwave designers use these simulators for their design problems but intensive computer time and memory requirements associated with the EM simulators have restricted their widespread use. Improvement of the performance/cost ratio for modern microwave filters requires manufacturing oriented design where full-wave tolerance analyses and yield optimization are required to be done which are computer-intensive. The ANN method of

14

modeling, optimization and design provides fast results and reduces the computational costs associated with that of time consuming EM solver.

(ii)   Usually several simulations are required to meet the filter specifications which takes considerable amount of time. In order to achieve filter specifications precisely, EM modeling is essential and minor tuning and adjustment in the post simulation fabrication process can help to meet the design goals. Generally iterations are done on the design parameters until desired response of the filters are realized. The whole process needs to be repeated with a slight change in any of the design specifications. These increases modeling time and complexity of hardware required for wireless and satellite communication. A faster method is needed to design this kind of devices including filters. ANN is a suitable technique for design and optimization of the same as compared to EM simulation. ANN model of a filter can be trained using the data from theoretical analysis and trained model of a filter can respond to unknown data within a specific accuracy for the designed frequency band.

It can approximate the filter response at a very modest fraction of the computer resources used by the commercial EM simulators. For optimization process using EM simulation tools a slight change in the physical dimensions requires a complete simulation which is time consuming and undesirable. Circuit response by analytical method is too slow whereas ANN based analytical models are fast and speed up the design process significantly. Once ANN models are developed for any device, these models can be used for design modification with suitable optimization algorithms. The usefulness of this approach in improving the efficiency and accuracy in the design process is already found in open literature [128-135]

.   Literature studies [141-144] has been done where fundamentals of ANN technique for RF and microwave design and its applications to design various devices used for microwave subsystem based on waveguide, planar (microstrip and strip line) as well as other configurations are discussed. The other useful application areas of ANN model are multilayer circuit design, CPW circuit design, design of printed antennas, and design of integrated circuit-antenna modules, design of active circuits and in high speed digital circuits. ANN response is reliable and accurate for all frequency points it is trained for and the computational cost associated to the modal analysis using EM simulation is 100 times more than that associated to the ANN model. This clarifies suitability of the use of a ANN model for intensively repetitive procedure. These aspects were the starting point for the present work.

1.3.4.4 GENETIC ALGORITHM (GA)/ PARTICLE SWARM OPTIMIZATION (PSO)

GA as an optimization method can be utilized to search the parameter space stochastically and generate solutions that are close to the optimal. The requirement of more iteration makes GA more computationally heavy and time consuming. PSO is another optimization algorithm easy to implement as there are fewer parameters to adjust. Another advantage of PSO is that there is no need for applying operators to the population; a process consumes time and memory storage.

AI techniques like GA/PSO can be extensively used for optimization of frequency response of microwave filters within a particular frequency band where EM simulation tools are not accessible and user defined specifications are required to be achieved within a short time. GA is generally used to search an optimal solution where the genetic composition of its population using different operations is modified until the solution becomes convergent. The GA is popular in academia and the industry mainly because of its intuitiveness, ease of implementation, and the ability to effectively solve highly nonlinear optimization problems of complex engineering systems [145-151].

PSO is a powerful Artificial Intelligence (AI) technique based on stochastic optimization and produces results in a faster, cheaper way compared with other evolutionary optimization methods [152-154].PSO is used to solve difficult or impossible numeric maximization and minimization problems in many research and application areas. PSO has better ability to search optimum solutions globally and is implemented in a wide range of research areas such as functional optimization, pattern recognition, NN training, fuzzy system control and obtained significant success.

1.4 OPTIMAL FILTER DESIGN

The following sections present topics and brief outline of the work done on which the present research work is carried out to acquaint the reader the reasons for choosing the same. Here 2D scattering from multiple dielectric posts in multilayer configuration inside rectangular waveguide is theoretically formulated using Lattice sum and T matrix technique and concept of image theory is used to derive frequency dependent S parameters of the same over different frequency points within X band. The theoretical computation using MATLAB is used to generate training/testing data for ANN model of the same and is used with GA optimization techniques for optimal design of VSWR BW and Band-Pass BW of the filter structure under consideration. A review of recently published literatures on application of AI techniques for optimization related problems [9] does not show any article similar to this particular work. These research findings are included in this thesis and details are covered in chapter 3 of the same.

Specifically the work is based on design and optimization of a waveguide filter where ANN model of the same is trained for different configuration of the multiple dielectric post loaded waveguide structure and the BPF response of the same is observed over the X band. Optimization of VSWR BW and Band-Pass BW of the filter is carried out using GA with appropriate fitness function. EM simulation of the rectangular waveguide structure having various combinations of dielectric posts inside the waveguide at X band is performed. Here commercially available software (HFSS) is used for verification of the VSWR BW and Band-Pass BW of BPF having 2x4 dielectric post configurations inside X band rectangular waveguide (Figure 1.7) and results are compared with that obtained from the ANN-GA model.

ii)   Another work on filter design and optimization based on Suspended Strip Line (SSL) configuration is carried out where broadside offset coupled resonator elements are used for synthesis of a broadband BPF (Figure 1.8).

Figure 1.5 3D view of rectangular waveguide having 2x4 dielectric post configuration

Figure 1.6 Waveguide BPF (a) SSL configuration (140 GHz), (b) Metal insert configuration (140 GHz) and (c) Inter-digital configuration (18 GHz - 40 GHz.)

Figure 1.7 2D view of SSL strip resonator of SSL Filter (a) top layer (b) bottom layer

Figure 1.8 3D view of microstrip ring filter

The SSL filters are lossless, light weight and fabrication cost of the structure is lower compared to that of waveguide filter. The filter parameters are modeled using ANN and GA is used for optimization of VSWR BW and Band-Pass BW in the frequency range 18.0 - 40.0 GHz.

iii)   One more investigation on microstrip ring filter where design and optimization of the same (Figure 1.9) using ANN-PSO model of the same is carried out for frequencies from 3.1GHz - 10.6 GHz. Objective of this work is to use the ANN model coupled with the PSO algorithm to synthesize the broadband microstrip filter using multiple rings and optimize its performance as a broadband filter in terms of frequency dependent S parameters. Here individual resonator elements are ring shaped and tuned using quarter wavelength short circuited stub. Trained ANN is used to model the nature of variation of S parameters of the individual ring resonator sections with its geometrical parameters and method of moment (MOM) has been used to generate data to train the ANN model of the same. Dimensions of ring resonators are computed from trained ANN model of the same and are used to design the integrated ring BPF using five such resonator sections. Optimization of integrated ring filter has been done using PSO for the entire frequency band 3.1GHz - 10.6 GHz. PSO is used in conjunction with the trained ANN model of resonator sections to optimize the integrated filter structure having five ring resonators and to modify the dimensions of the same for obtaining wideband performance of the BPF under consideration.

For verification of frequency response of S parameters of filters under consideration EM simulation tools are used. In this thesis mainly HFSS (3D Maxwell EM simulator based on FEM) is used to model periodic structure having symmetry conditions on the boundaries. Another popular MOM based EM simulator (IE3D) is used in this thesis for theoretical analysis and verification process.

1.5. SIMULATION TECHNIQUES USED FOR FILTER

Analytical techniques to predict EM behavior of any passive devices includes (i) asymptotic analysis (ii) variation analysis, (iii) integral transforms, (iv) contour integration, and (v) perturbation theory. Improvements in computer speed and memory helped to develop some analytical methods known as Computational Electro-Magnetic (CEM) methods, Finite Element (FE) method, Finite Difference Time Domains (FDTD), Finite Difference Frequency Domains (FDFD) methods, Transmission line matrix (TLM) method, Method of Moments (MOM), Mode-Matching method (MMM), Finite Integral Technique (FIT) are widely used in the characterization of waveguide structures. These methods, separately or combined, can be used to simulate the waveguide structures, but all of them consume excessive time of central processing unit (CPU).

In order to optimize a filter, theoretical design processes, synthesis steps, analysis process and different optimization techniques useful for optimal design of filters are avaiable in open literature [124-135]. The use of an optimization algorithm has to be done efficiently in order to avoid the local minima of complicated error functions defined to reach optimal design of the filter under considerations.

In house developed MATLAB [140] code has been used in this thesis to implement GA/ANN/PSO technique for filter optimization. Commercially available software HFSS based on FEM and IE3D based on MOM has been used to validate the frequency response of optimal filters obtained from GA/ANN/PSO techniques.

1.6 FABRICATION TECHNIQUES FOR FILTER

Waveguide filters are used for both narrow-band and wide-band applications. Several fabrication techniques involving different degrees of accuracy and costs can be used for development of the hardware for filters based on waveguide structures. Satellite applications demand very high-precision components, where dimensional tolerances are usually required to be below 10 μm. Spark eroding or electroforming are usually expensive techniques but useful for accurate fabrication. Comparatively low-cost manufacturing methods, CNC (computer-controlled) milling or die-casting, can perturb the electrical response of the filter.

Microwave filters for space systems are traditionally implemented with waveguide technology, mainly due to low losses and high power handling capability. Waveguide structures are typically bulky, to reduce the mass and volume of the structure under consideration, weighty materials like aluminum can be replaced by lighter ones, like Kevlar (composed of lightweight plastic fibers).The use of graphite waveguides or carbon fiber technology is preferred and for efficient use of these lighter materials, a deposit of high conductivity silver onto them is required to achieve the good conductor properties for the waveguide walls.

The fabrication of optimized SSL BPF and rectangular waveguide BPF having of 2x4 post configuration has been done using milling technology. The optimal ring filter has been fabricated using photo-lithography techniques and bonding of connectors/flanges as a pre measurement process has also been carried out.

1.7. FILTER MEASUREMENT PROCEDURE

Complete characterization (swept-frequency measurements) of filters at microwave frequencies can be done using Vector Network Analyzers (VNA). The frequency response of a filter includes transmission response and reflection response. The most commonly measured filter characteristics are Insertion Loss (I.L.), Return Loss (R.L.), VSWR BW, transmission BW and out-of-band rejection. These parameters are used to measure how well a filter passes signals within its band of operation while simultaneously rejecting signals outside that band. During measurement of VSWR BW and Band-Pass BW of fabricated filters under study minimum criterion for evaluation of performance of the same has been set as $S_{11} < -3.0$ dB and $S_{21} > -3.0$ dB.

1.8 ORGANIZATION OF THE THESIS

The research work carried out for this thesis is solely based on ANN modeling of filters and are implemented in waveguide, microstrip and SSL configuration. Investigations on optimal design of three different filters are done using soft computing techniques like GA or PSO for filter response over a broad frequency band and details are included in this thesis. Design, optimization and frequency response of S parameters of three different BPF structures are discussed in this thesis where ANN models, GA techniques, PSO optimization technique are utilized to develop optimal BPF in place the conventional design/ optimization process using EM simulation. Here one multi-post rectangular waveguide structure, one SSL structure and one mictrostrip stub tuned ring structure has been considered. Design and optimization are carried out and VSWR and Band-Pass BW of each of the BPF configuration are optimized using AI techniques. The aim is to obtain optimal design of the filters within the frequency band under consideration and to replace use of EM simulator with soft computing algorithm for predicting performance of the BPF structures chosen to carry out research.

The overall thesis is divided into six chapters. Chapter 1 consists of a small introduction followed by different sections on optimal design of filters, AI techniques and motivation of work, scope of work and organization of this thesis. In addition a brief review on filter design, different types of filter configurations, elaborate discussion on filter application are included in chapter 1 of this thesis.

The research work is based on theoretical analysis using scattering (S) theory involving Lattice Sum and T-matrix which are used to formulate the expressions for frequency dependent reflectance and transmittance of multi-post rectangular waveguide structure. Code using MATLAB is developed to compute the same for different combination of the dielectric posts inside rectangular waveguide where post parameters and waveguide dimensions are varied for design of BPF/BSF. The theory and mathematical formulations using multidimensional matrices where 2D scattering of periodic dielectric and metallic structures inside rectangular waveguide using Lattice Sum and T-matrix approach [155-158] are considered to find out reflection and transmission coefficients of a single post or layer of posts uniformly spaced inside rectangular waveguides. The mathematical expressions where algebraic manipulation are used for deriving expression for S parameters of the multiple post rectangular waveguide structure as given in Appendix of this thesis.

The effect of positional and dimensional parameters of dielectric posts on VSWR BW and transmission BW of the rectangular waveguide filter has been investigated in details using ANN model of the same. Plots showing the effects of post radii, post dielectric constants, inter-post separation, inter-layer separation on reflectance and transmittance of the filter structure using 2x4 post configuration inside X band rectangular waveguide are included in chapter 2 of this thesis. The detail design of rectangular waveguide filter having different configuration of dielectric posts where frequency response of S-parameters of the same are computed and studied for its utility as broadband BPF are also discussed in chapter 2 of this thesis.

The application of ANN to model EM scattering of cylindrical posts inside rectangular waveguide is discussed in chapter 2 of this thesis. ANN model of multi-post rectangular waveguide filter is trained using the data available from the theoretical analysis (using T-matrix and Lattice Sum techniques) to compute frequency response of reflectance and transmittance of multiple post rectangular waveguide structure and details are included in chapter 2. The frequency response of the trained ANN model of a rectangular waveguide having single conducting post, single dielectric post and four dielectric posts are reported by the author and details are shown in chapter 2 of this thesis. Filter configuration having multiple posts inside rectangular waveguide with uniform /non uniform radius and separation arranged as per Chebyshev or Gaussian distribution is also studied using EM simulation and details are included in chapter 2 of this thesis.

The research topic in this thesis is based on optimal design of waveguide filter where a rectangular waveguide structure having multiple posts are used to compute frequency responses of S-parameters of the same and further optimization to get better frequency responses in terms of VSWR BW and Band-Pass BW. Here AI techniques are utilized to compute frequency responses of optimal filter and measurement has been done using developed BPF to verify the utility of the AI technique for optimal design of filters in place of EM simulation tools. The technical details of design, simulation results and measurement results of waveguide BPF along with other two different BPF structures have been included in chapter 3-5 of this thesis.

In chapter 3 ANN model of a rectangular waveguide structure having 2x4 post configurations is discussed. The structure under consideration is designed using trained (using scattering theory) ANN model of the same to work as BPF at X band and optimized using GA to get broadband frequency response of S parameters of the same. Frequency response performance of the optimal waveguide filter is verified using EM simulation. The procedures of optimization, EM simulation results and measured results of the BPF are discussed in details in chapter 3 of this thesis. Finally experimental verification (with reasonable accuracy) process which establish the usefulness of AI procedure for optimal design of the multi-post rectangular waveguide filter has been discussed in details and included in chapter 3 of this thesis.

Chapter 4 consists of optimal design, development details of a BPF in Suspended Strip Line (SSL) form. The requirement of broadband filter in the 18.0-40.0 GHz. frequency range is for commercial use. Few manufacturing companies like REACTEL INC, KL MICROWAVE, YIG MICROLAMDA WIRELESS INC have already launched filters having pass band as 18.0-40.0 GHz. The filter under consideration is synthesized using SSL medium and the ANN model of this filter is trained in the frequency range 18.0 GHz - 40.0 GHz. using theoretically computed data (spectral domain analysis). Here the trained ANN model is used to design the optimal SSL filter where optimizations of frequency dependent S parameters of the same are carried out using GA algorithm. Here this type of filter is developed for research purpose where AI techniques are used to optimize the VSWR BW and Band-Pass BW of the same. The fabricated broadband BPF using SSL structure is measured to compare its performance with that using EM simulation and details are included in chapter 4 of this thesis.

The design of an optimal ring filter using microstrip structure where ANN-PSO technique is applied is described in chapter 5 of this thesis. Here ANN model of the individual sections of the filter is designed and trained properly using theoretically computed data (MOM). EM simulation tools are used to verify the performance of trained ANN model of individual section of the filter structure under consideration. The purpose is to predict the frequency response of that filter over the frequency band without using EM simulation. The final dimensions of the optimal BPF are computed using ANN-PSO algorithm where five such ring resonators are used and measured VSWR BW and Band-Pass BW of the optimized ring filter are compared with that of the simulated one. The usefulness of ANN-PSO algorithm is thus established here for design of optimal microstrip stub tuned ring filter where VSWR BW and Band-Pass BW has been optimized. The technical details design, optimization procedure and measurement results are included in chapter 5 of this thesis.

Finally the thesis is concluded with future scope or work in chapter 6. This chapter has a brief summary on work done so far and reported results. In this thesis design/development stages of three different structures are covered where AI techniques are used to design an optimal BPF and measurement results to validate the design procedure. Theoretical investigations using EM analysis are done to compute design data for development of the trained ANN model of the each BPF. Mathematical codes are developed to generate adequate numerical data to train and test ANN model of the respective BPF configurations. An equivalent model of the structure is thus generated where the input / output parameters obtained from the model is further optimized to design broadband BPF.

1.9 SUMMARY

In this chapter optimal design of filters using different band-pass structures are discussed. It has been shown that the trained ANN model with suitable optimization program using GA/PSO can yield a faster and accurate filter solution. Instead of using computer intensive EM simulation tools the artificial computation technique are more suitable to model selected parameters of any passive device over a frequency band of interest. In the latter case the optimization process is not computers intensive and easy mathematical codes can be developed to get optimal design of the device under consideration. However the designer should adopt a proper optimization process to fulfill the requirement of accuracy of specifications of the filter for any particular application.

Brief discussions on basic ideas of filters, techniques for optimal design of filters, motivation of work, scope of work, organization of this thesis, author's contribution are discussed in chapter 1. Detail discussions about AI techniques and their applications in different BPFs are included in subsequent chapters to get a clear picture of work done by the author and basis of publications made so far. Efforts are made to establish applications of soft computing techniques in filter design for completing this thesis and new findings are published. The thesis is completed with experimental results for performance verifications of the developed filters which establish the usefulness of AI techniques in design and optimization of waveguide filters and other printed filters.

Detail design procedure of multi-post waveguide filter using ANN technique and its optimization process using GA are included in chapter 3 of this thesis. In addition design and optimization process of one SSL filter and one microstrip ring filter has been discussed using trained models and soft computing algorithms. Verifications of the filter performances by EM simulation, measured performances, comparison with that of the optimal design are carried out and included in chapter 4-5 of this thesis. Details of work done so far and published papers are included in this thesis where the goal is to establish proof of concept and industrial/military levels of precision desired has not been attempted at all.

2

ANN TECHNIQUE FOR DESIGN OF WAVEGUIDE FILTER WITH DIELECTRIC POSTS AND EFFECTS OF DESIGN PARAMETERS ON FILTER PERFORMANCE

2.1 INTRODUCTION

Periodic dielectric or metallic structures inside a waveguide are very useful [16-17] for their wide applications in microwave frequency regions. Recent literature survey [18-21] shows different analysis methods for structures having periodic dielectric posts arranged inside waveguide. The EM scattering of a plane wave from a cylindrical object as shown in Figure 2.1 can be theoretically formulated [22-23] for a multi-post multi-layer rectangular waveguide at X band. The trained and tested ANN model of the structure under consideration is very useful to study the characteristics of the same within a frequency band and design/optimization of frequency response of S parameters using trained ANN model of the same can be done using soft computing algorithm as shown in subsequent chapters.

Scattering theory [157-159] is utilized to compute frequency dependent S-parameter data of multi-post multi-layer rectangular waveguide which has been used to develop trained and tested ANN model of the same. Frequency response of reflectance and transmittance of the filter structure having 2x4 post configuration inside X band rectangular waveguide is also computed theoretically using EM simulation for comparison with the responses computed from its developed ANN model.

The effects of positional and dimensional parameters of dielectric post on frequency response of S parameters of the filter structure under consideration and relative effects on filter performances have been investigated in detail and included in this chapter. The 2x4 post configuration inside X band rectangular waveguide has been used to study the same for different sets of parameters of dielectric posts and has been utilized here for optimal design of the BPF.

It is observed that BP or BS responses are possible outcome from multi-post multi-layer rectangular waveguide depending on suitable physical parameters like radius, dielectric constant, inter-post/inter-layer spacing and configuration of dielectric posts where frequency of operation/waveguide dimensions also plays major role. It is observed that frequency response of S parameters of a structure having multi-post multi-layer configuration inside rectangular waveguide can be designed as BPF having broad VSWR BW and Band- Pass BW if design parameters of the same are computed in a systematic way. The optimal design of a filter is possible if the trained ANN model of the same is utilized with an optimization algorithm to compute the design parameters of the filter structure under consideration.

Outlines of the theoretical background, development of ANN model of the structure, training and testing procedure are included in this chapter. Theoretical investigation using scattering theory, development of trained ANN model and verification by EM simulation have been carried out on few multi-post rectangular waveguide configurations where emphasis has been made to extract filter responses, enhancement of VSWR BW and Band-Pass BW of the filter and optimization of the frequency response of reflectance and transmittance of the same.

Here AI techniques are utilized to obtain the optimized frequency response of S parameters of multi-post multi-layer rectangular waveguide structure. The physical parameters of the multi-post multi-layer rectangular waveguide structure for optimal BPF response are tabulated and fabrication, measurements and verifications are carried out to establish usefulness of AI techniques for optimal design of BPF in place of EM simulator.

2.2 ANALYSIS OF ELECTRO-MAGNETIC (EM) SCATTERING FROM MULTI-POST WAVEGUIDE

Here the research work is carried out on rectangular waveguide structure having multiple dielectric posts arranged in a uniform/non uniform manner as shown in Figure 2.1-2.2. The aim is to study EM scattering from multiple dielectric posts inside rectangular waveguide structure where scattering theory involving Lattice Sum and T-matrix [155-158] techniques are utilized.

The EM scattering from dielectric post configuration inside rectangular waveguide are formulated theoretically and used to compute frequency depended reflectance and transmittance of the structure. The effect of design parameters of the structure under consideration has been investigated in details and the effect of post parameters (dimension/position) on frequency dependent reflectance and transmittance of the same are studied as far as possible.

It is observed that the frequency depended transmittance and reflectance of the structure under consideration can be designed as BPF when parameters of dielectric posts are properly selected. It is also observed that BPF responses can be optimized for a particular frequency band using optimization algorithm where a set of parameters of dielectric posts are selected for design of optimal BPF. It is also observed that BPF and BSF responses can be synthesized using non uniform arrangement of multiple dielectric posts in multilayer configuration inside rectangular waveguide and by varying the post parameters in a systematic way [159-160]. The details of observations on nature of variation of design parameters, their effects of VSWR BW and Band-Pass BW of the configuration under consideration are made and included in this chapter. Here studied using EM simulation and developed ANN model of the same are utilized for optimal design of the filter structure under consideration.

2.2.1 CONFIGURATIONS OF MULTI-POST MULTI-LAYERED WAVEGUIDE

The frequency responses of S parameters of a rectangular waveguide having multiple dielectric posts in multilayer configuration are studied for the following cases.

(i)   Two dielectric posts inside rectangular waveguide having uniform separation and radius in two post single layer configuration forming BP responses as shown in Figure 2.2(a)

(ii)   Four dielectric posts inside rectangular waveguide having uniform separation and radius in two post two layer configuration forming BP responses as shown in Figure 2.2(b)

(iii)   Eight dielectric posts inside rectangular waveguide having uniform separation and radius in two post four layer configuration forming BP responses as shown in Figure 2.2(c)

(iv)   Twelve dielectric posts inside rectangular waveguide having uniform separation and radius in two post six layer configuration forming BP/BS responses as shown in Figure 2.2(d)

(v)   Sixteen dielectric posts inside rectangular waveguide having uniform separation and radius in two post eight layer configuration forming BP/BS responses as shown in Figure 2.2(e), 2.5(a)

(vi)   Thirty two dielectric posts inside rectangular waveguide having uniform separation and uniform radius in two post sixteen layer configuration to form BP responses as shown in Figure 2.2(f)

(vii)   Sixteen dielectric posts inside rectangular waveguide having varying radius and uniform separation according to Cheyshev distribution in two post eight layer configurations to form BP responses as shown in Figure 2.5(b).

(viii) Sixteen dielectric posts inside rectangular waveguide having varying radius and non uniform separation according to Gaussian distribution in two post eight layer configurations to form BP responses as shown in Figure 2.5(c).

Theoretical analysis of a structure having periodic array of vertical cylindrical posts in a rectangular waveguide and their applications as filter is the main topic of discussions of this chapter. Multiple dielectric post configuration arranged in a periodic manner inside a rectangular waveguide as shown in Figure 2.2 is useful for design of filters in microwave and millimeter wave bands. The nature of variation of transmittance and reflectance of the filter configuration under consideration are observed to be depended on parameters of dielectric posts at the frequency of operation. Here in depth studies on this topic are carried out where frequency dependent S parameters of the structure obtained from theoretical computations are verified using EM simulation and are discussed in detail in the next sections.

2.2.2 ANALYSIS OF RECTANGULAR WAVEGUIDE WITH FULL HEIGHT CYLINDRICAL POSTS

A rigorous semi-analytical approach is considered to formulate mathematically the problem of scattering from vertical full-height cylindrical posts inside a rectangular waveguide (shown in Figure 2.1(a)-(b)). The problem is transformed into a problem of 2D scattering of a plane wave by a periodic array of circular cylinders using the image theory [15-21]. A vertical full height post from the top wall to the bottom wall of a rectangular waveguide when combined with its mirror images [23] (with respect to two side walls) can be considered as a periodic array of parallel cylinders, The reflection and transmission matrices, which characterize scattering from post array, can be written using closed form expressions based on the Lattice Sum technique [156-158] and the T-matrix of a circular cylinder isolated in free space.

The formulations for the reflection and transmission matrices on the basis of waveguide modes due to pair of posts inside the guide can be expressed as closed form algebraic equations. The frequency responses of S parameters of the structure having array of posts inside rectangular waveguide can thus be computed using the reflection and transmission matrices.

The rectangular waveguide structure having single layer two post configurations as shown in Figure 2.3(a) is considered for theoretical analysis. When the posts are stacked along the waveguide, the original post and an infinite number of images as shown in Figure 2.3(b) are considered for computation of S matrices and the reflection and transmission matrices defined for each pair of posts are successively concatenated using the recurrence relations. This leads to the generalized reflection and transmission matrices of the structure formed by the array of two posts along the waveguide and can be used to design frequency response of the same as BPF for proper choice of parameters of the structure.

This approach can also be used to analyze a waveguide configuration having N stacked pair with 2N number of dielectric posts where the position, radius and dielectric constant for each of the 2N posts are considered as independent parameters. It is observed that frequency responses can be obtained from the multi-post waveguide configuration under consideration by controlling these parameters in a systematic way. The reflection and transmission matrices of the structure are computed using aggregate T matrices and Lattice Sum techniques. With successive concatenation generalized reflection and transmission matrices are computed which characterize the frequency response of an N stacked pair of two posts in the rectangular waveguide.

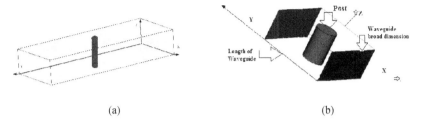

(a)   (b)

Figure 2.1 3D views of rectangular waveguide with single full height post (a) schematic view (b) enlarged view

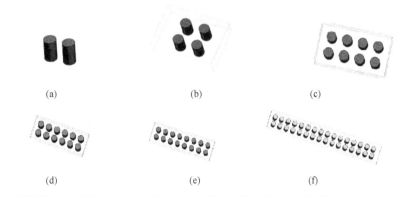

(a)   (b)   (c)

(d)   (e)   (f)

Figure 2.2 3D views of dielectric post configuration (uniform radius and spacing) inside rectangular waveguide
(a) 1x2 (b) 2x2 (c) 2x4 d) 2x6, e) 2x8, f) 2x16

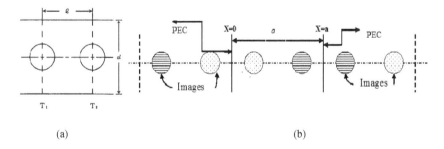

(a)   (b)

Figure 2.3 Two post configuration inside rectangular waveguide a) top view, b) cross sections of series of images along broad dimension of waveguide

The analysis of the structures under consideration using rigorous methods can yield highly accurate results but at the expense of considerable analytical efforts for complicated computer programming. As per literature [128-135] ANN method of modeling bypasses the repeated use of

28

complex iterative process and the model designed for desired accuracy within a frequency band are accurate enough for practical realization of the frequency responses of the structure under consideration.

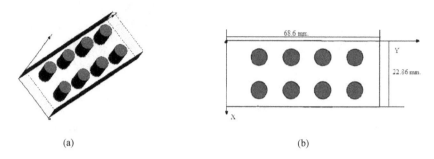

(a)   (b)

Figure 2.4 X band waveguide having dielectric full height posts in 2x4 configurations (a) 3D view (b) 2D view

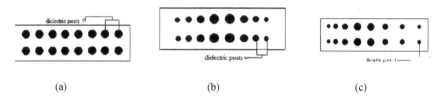

(a)   (b)   (c)

Figure 2.5 Cross section of multilayer dielectric post configuration inside rectangular waveguide a) Sixteen dielectric posts (2x8) having uniform radius and uniform separation, b) Sixteen dielectric posts(2x8) having uniform separation and non uniform radius varying according to Chebyshev distribution, c) Sixteen dielectric posts(2x8) having varying radius and non uniform separation according to Gaussian distribution.

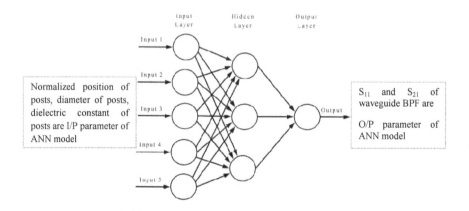

Figure 2.6 ANN model of waveguide filter having input and output parameters

Computation using EM analysis methods requires costly resources which are essential to predict accurate frequency responses of the structure under consideration. Analysis results obtained using EM simulators are comparable to that obtained using trained ANN model within the frequency band under consideration.

2.3 AI TECHNIQUE FOR DESIGN OF RECTANGULAR WAVEGUIDE FILTER

Set of post parameters are used to design frequency responses of multi-post rectangular waveguide structure as BPF at the frequency band under consideration. A trained ANN model of the structure under consideration are utilized with optimization techniques for design/development of optimal BPF and parameters of the same are modified to obtain broad VSWR BW and Band-Pass BW of the same over a frequency band. Here the trained ANN model of multi-post rectangular waveguide structure is used with GA optimizer for computation of optimum transmittance and reflectance of the BPF and EM simulation is used to cross check the computed results.

2.4 ANN MODEL OF CONDUCTING / DIELECTRIC POST INSIDE A RECTANGULAR WAVEGUIDE

Here focus is made on the use of AI technique (ANN) for modeling input/output relationship of a rectangular waveguide having conducting/dielectric post configuration. ANN is used here for non-linear modeling of the frequency response of structures having single/multiple cylindrical conducting /dielectric posts in a 3D rectangular waveguide as shown in Figure 2.1-2.2.

Frequency dependent S parameters of the multi-post multi-layer rectangular waveguide structure under consideration are computed using semi-analytical formulations based on Image theory, T-matrix and Lattice Sum techniques as included in Appendix where self written MATLAB code is used to compute the same using a set of mathematical expressions [23,159-160].

2.4.1 DESIGN OF ANN MODEL

In this process an ANN model of the multi-post rectangular waveguide is designed, trained / tested to the desired degree of accuracy using the numerical values of design parameters of posts, dimensions of waveguide and frequency dependent S parameters of the structure under consideration. The trained and tested ANN model can be used to find out frequency dependent S_{21} and S_{11} for multi-post multi-layer waveguide filter configurations for different sets of post parameters at specific frequency bands. Details of design and simulation results are discussed in next sections of this chapter.

2.4.2 TRAINING AND DEVELOPMENT OF ANN MODEL

For a frequency band of interest (X band) mathematical computation of S parameters for the structure having single/multiple post configuration inside rectangular waveguide is performed using MATLAB code. Frequency depended S_{11} and S_{21} data for the structure are generated and 80% of them are used for proper training of the ANN model of the same. Rest of the data generated is used for testing the model for the required accuracy. Here the gradient descent back propagation model is used for minimizing the error function. The resulting mean squared error between the network output and target values over all training pairs are minimized.

Table 2.1 shows the training and testing accuracies of the ANN model of the waveguide filter. Trained/tested ANN model of cylindrical full height post configuration (single/multiple) inside rectangular waveguide is used here to compute the frequency response of the S parameters of the same at X band for single conducting post and single / multiple dielectric post configurations. Frequency responses of the S parameters computed from trained ANN model are observed and compared with those computed theoretically as shown in Figures 2.7-2.9.

2.4.2.1 SINGLE CONDUCTING POST

A three layer MLP is used to model the scattering from conducting full height post made of brass having radius 0.7 mm. inside rectangular waveguide as shown in Figure 2.1. Here the post position relative to two axes of the waveguide and its radius are taken as inputs of ANN model. The waveguide used here is WR-90 (22.85 mm. x 10.16 mm.) for X band of frequencies. The number of neurons taken for the hidden layer is 48. Training data generated from the theoretical analysis of EM scattering has a normalized range from -1 to +1, the bipolar sigmoid function is chosen as activation function. The ANN model is trained using 125 data sets involving various combinations of normalized parameters of post positions and its radii.

2.4.2.2 SINGLE DIELECTRIC POST

The ANN model for single dielectric vertical full height post (having dielectric constant 9.8, radius 3.4 mm) placed centrally inside rectangular waveguide is considered as shown in Figure 2.1. A suitable combination of array of such posts inside rectangular waveguide can be arranged and parameters of the same are selected for application of the structure as filter. The ANN model of the same is used here to design/optimize performance of the structure. Here two input parameters (diameter of dielectric post and dielectric constant normalized with respect to their respective maximum values) are assigned to two neurons in the input layers. Frequency responses of the S-parameters of the structure (magnitude and phase normalized with respect to their respective maximum values) are assigned as two output parameters and represented by two neurons in the output layer. A four layer MLP is used with two hidden layers having 36 and 32 neurons respectively for the design of ANN model of the structure having single dielectric vertical full height post inside X band rectangular waveguide. The training data generated from the theoretical analysis has normalized range from -1 to +1 and the bipolar sigmoid function is chosen as activation function. The ANN model is trained using 550 data sets involving various combinations of normalized input parameters.

2.4.2.3 EIGHT (2X4) DIELECTRIC POSTS

A four layer MLP is used to model the scattering from 2x4 full-height cylindrical dielectric post configuration inside X band rectangular waveguide as shown in Figure 2.2(c). The post positions are chosen to be symmetric with respect to both axis of the waveguide for application of the structure under consideration as filter. The input layer has four independent neurons which represent four input parameters normalized with respect to their respective maximum values. For the purpose of training of ANN model diameter of the posts, positions of post (the other two are symmetrically placed) relative to both axis of the waveguide and dielectric constants of the post material are taken as inputs. The two hidden layers are chosen having 48 and 28 number of neurons respectively. The output layer has two neurons representing magnitude (S_{11}) and magnitude (S_{21}) normalized with respect to their maximum values. The waveguide used here is WR-90 (22.86 mm. x 10.16 mm.) for the X band of frequencies. The training data generated from the EM scattering analysis (using Lattice Sum and T matrix) has a normalized range from -1 to $+1$, the bipolar sigmoid function is chosen as activation function. The ANN model is trained using 1310 data sets involving various combinations of normalized input parameters.

2.5 TESTING OF ANN MODEL OF POST CONFIGURATION INSIDE RECTANGULAR WAVEGUIDE

Trained ANN model of multi-post multi-layer rectangular waveguide structures are developed where the theoretical data using computation techniques [155-158] are used (discussed in Appendix of this thesis). The training and testing accuracies of ANN model for single conducting/dielectric/multiple dielectric posts inside an X band rectangular waveguide are dependent on the number of neurons in each layer, number of training data, target accuracy and convergence criteria used. Here the training accuracy of S_{11} is set as 0.1 and that of S_{21} is set as 0.05 for the ANN model of single conducting/dielectric/multiple dielectric posts inside an X band rectangular waveguide.

Here three different ANN models of rectangular waveguide having single/multiple posts are developed and trained using the data obtained from EM analysis involving Lattice Sum and T matrix. The output parameters of tested ANN models are compared with the theoretically obtained S parameters of the rectangular waveguide structure having single/multiple posts inside it and the plots for the respective cases are shown in the Figure 2.7-2.9 for comparison. Table 2.1 shows training and testing accuracy of trained ANN model of rectangular waveguide having single/multiple posts obtained for output parameters of the same. The testing of the ANN models is carried out using known data sets which are not used in the training process.

2.5.1 SINGLE CONDUCTING POST

After proper training the average error of S-parameters is found to be 0.001 over a set of test data spanning the entire X band of frequencies and different values for the position and radii of the scattering post as shown in Figure 2.7(a)-2.7(b), ensuring that the testing data are not used in the training process.

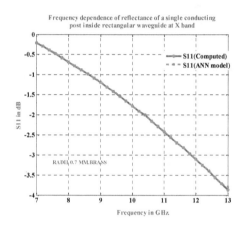

(a)

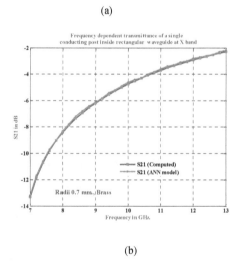

(b)

Figure 2.7 Frequency responses of S parameters of X band rectangular waveguide having single conducting post (radii 0.7 mm) a) S_{11} b) S_{21}

2.5.2 SINGLE DIELECTRIC POST

After proper training the average relative error is found to be 0.1 for S_{11} (magnitude) and 0.05 for S_{21} (magnitude) over a test data set spanning the entire X band of frequencies and different values for the position and dielectric constant of the dielectric post as shown in Figure 2.8(a)-2.8(b), which are not used in the training process.

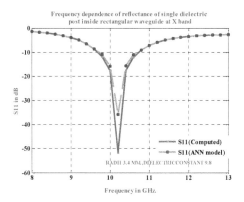

(a)

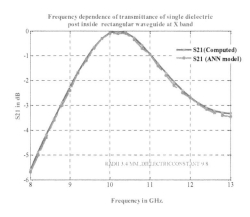

(b)

Figure 2.8 Frequency responses of S parameters of X band rectangular waveguide having single dielectric post (radii 3.0, dielectric constant 12.0) a) S_{11} b) S_{21}

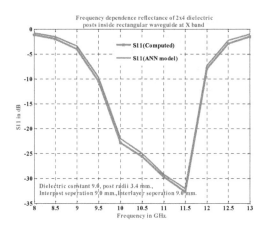

(a)

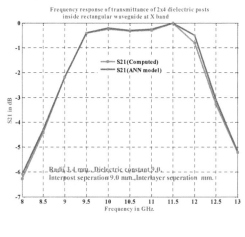

(b)

Figure 2.9 Frequency responses of S parameters of X band rectangular waveguide having 2x4 post configuration (radii 3.4 mm, dielectric constant 9.0, inter-post/inter-layer separation 9.0 mm a) S_{11}, b) S_{21}

2.5.3 EIGHT (2X4) DIELECTRIC POSTS

After proper training the average relative error is found to be 0.1 for S_{11} (magnitude) and 0.05 for S_{21} (magnitude) over a set of test data spanning the entire X band of frequencies and different values for the post diameter, post position and dielectric constant as shown in Figure 2.9 (a)-2.9 (b), which are not used in the training process. It is observed that for eight dielectric post in 2x4 configuration inside X band rectangular waveguide the trained NN model is found to be working within the error boundary limited by the practical measurement error of S_{11} (magnitude) and S_{21} (magnitude).

Using the trained ANN model time consuming EM simulation process can be eliminated, within a desired accuracy the frequency response of the waveguide filter can be predicted using the trained ANN model used for this work. The main purpose of using ANN model is to observe filter response by varying parameters of the posts used to design multi-post rectangular waveguide structure and optimization process can be incorporated further.

2.6 AI TECHNIQUES FOR DESIGN AND OPTIMIZATION OF WAVEGUIDE BPF

It is observed that parameters of dielectric posts plays significant role in design of the multi-post multi-layer waveguide BPF. Frequency response of S parameters of the structure under consideration is directly related to the post parameters. Synthesis of filter response for a particular waveguide within a frequency band is dependent on parameters like post radii, inter-post separation, inter layer separation and gap of centre of post from edge of waveguide side walls. It has been studied that the frequency response of S parameters of the BPF configuration under consideration can be optimized using soft computing algorithm with proper fitness function. A suitable optimization algorithm can be used to compute optimal design of the multi-post multi-layer waveguide configuration under study where the physical and positional parameters of dielectric posts are modified in a systematic way.

2.6.1 ANN MODEL OF MULTI-LAYER MULTI-POST RECTANGULAR WAVEGUIDE

The structure having multiple dielectric posts in multi-layer configuration inside rectangular waveguide has been replaced by an artificial model and further design /optimization steps are followed using the processed model. Here ANN model of rectangular waveguide structure having multi-post multi-layer configurations has been designed and a suitable input/output parameter set associated with the model is processed (trained) using mathematical tools. It is observed that within a reasonable accuracy the frequency response of S parameters of waveguide filter can be predicted using trained ANN model of the same and time consuming EM simulation process can be eliminated.

The main purpose of using trained ANN model is to i) observe frequency response of the multi-post multi-layer rectangular waveguide structure by varying post parameters and further optimization of selected input/output parameters of the same ii) study the effect of dimensional and positional parameters of dielectric posts on frequency dependent transmittance and reflectance of multi-post rectangular waveguide structure without using EM simulation tools iii) compare the frequency response performances of multi-post multi-layer rectangular waveguide structures having 2x2, 2x4, 2x6, 2x8 post configurations at X band.

36

It is observed that the frequency responses of S parameters of the BPF structures under consideration can be obtained within a specified frequency band and broad VSWR and Band-Pass BW of the filter configuration under consideration can be obtained using optimization algorithm for specific set of post parameters. In this process numbers of layers are varied and natures of variations of VSWR BW, Transmission BW and physical sizes for each multi-post (2x2, 2x4, 2x6, and 2x8) BPF structure under consideration is observed using trained ANN model of the same as shown in Figures 2.10(a)-(b). The effect of dielectric constant of posts on transmittance of the structure under consideration is shown in Figure 2.11 and It has been observed that the variation of S_{21} of the same with frequency is non linear in nature, increases significantly for higher values of dielectric constants.

16 cylindrical dielectric posts in 2x8 configurations inside X band rectangular waveguide having uniform inter-layer spacing and inter-post spacing are studied and it is observed that training process of the corresponding ANN model requires time to converge with the desired accuracy, due to limitations of computational resources. So techniques of optimization using EM simulation tools, trained ANN model combined with soft computing algorithm and other standard techniques can be used purposefully for optimal design of filters and it is solely dependent on specific applications, available resources and accuracies of results required.

2.7 STUDIES ON EFFECTS OF DESIGN PARAMETERS ON FREQUENCY RESPONSE OF BPF

Here extensive studies are made on effects of different parameters of dielectric posts on VSWR BW and Transmission BW of rectangular waveguide having multiple posts in multilayer configuration. Effects of each parameter on VSWR BW and Band-Pass BW of the BPF are studied in detail and are included in this chapter of this thesis. Post parameters like radius, dielectric constant, inter-post spacing, interlayer spacing etc are varied and frequency response of S parameters of the BPF configuration under consideration are computed using trained /tested ANN model of a 2x4 post configuration inside rectangular waveguide at X band. Emphasis has been given here to find out

i) Influence of post parameters on nature of variation of frequency response of S parameters the BPF

ii) Effect of post parameters on design/optimization of the BPF

iii) Observation of factors that imposes practical limitations to implement optimal design.

The rectangular waveguide structure having dielectric posts arranged in 2x4 array configuration having two posts per layer with uniform separation as shown in Figure 2.2(c) is considered here. A parametric study using X band rectangular waveguide having 2x4 post configuration is done where effects of post radii, dielectric constant, inter post spacing and interlayer spacing on frequency response of S parameters of the same is investigated. It has been found that synthesis of BPF response using multi-post multi-layer waveguide is dependent on design parameters

37

like post radii, inter-post separation, inter-layer separation and gap of centre of post from edge of waveguide side walls.

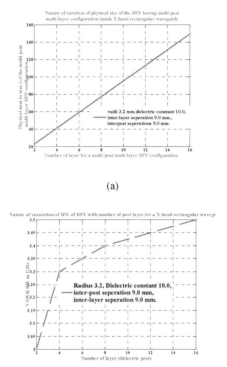

(a)

(b)

Figure 2.10 Nature of variation of VSWR BW of the filter configuration having multi-post multi-layer rectangular waveguide at X band where effects of (a) size of BPF (b) addition of post layers are considered

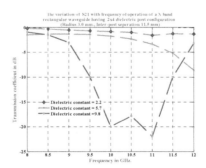

Figure 2.11 Effects of dielectric constant of posts on S_{21} of 2x4 post configuration inside X band rectangular waveguide

38

It has been studied that the frequency response of S parameters of the BPF configuration can be designed within the operating frequency band of the waveguide and parameters of dielectric posts plays significant role in design of the BPF/optimization of the same. Here trained ANN model of the 2x4 post configuration uniformly spaced inside rectangular waveguide is used to compute range of post parameters where frequency responses of reflectance and transmittance of the structure under consideration will be like a BPF and which can further be optimized using soft computing algorithm. Here GA is used for performance enhancement of frequency response of S parameters of BPF structure under consideration and EM simulation is used to compare the accuracies of design/optimization of frequency response of S parameters of the same.

This study in turn facilities choice of post parameters from the range computed and using trained ANN model of the multi-post multi-layer rectangular waveguide structure optimal design of BPF can be obtained as per requirement. Here EM simulations tools are used to compare the accuracies of computed design/optimized results. BW enhancement of filter structures under consideration in terms of $|S_{21}|$ and $|S_{11}|$ of the same are depended on parameters of posts and the studies made so far can be utilized to estimate the practical range of VSWR BW and Band-Pass BW possible to achieve using 2x4 post configuration inside X band rectangular waveguide.

2.7.1 RANGE OF POST PARAMETERS FOR DESIGN OF BROADBAND BPF

Here studies are made on variation of frequency dependent S parameters of 2x4 post configuration inside rectangular waveguide when dimensions of post parameters are varied. Here trained ANN model of the structure under consideration is used to study frequency dependent S parameters of the same where dimensions of post parameters are varied.

Observations on i) nature of filter response using 2x4 post configuration inside rectangular waveguide, ii) effects of post parameters on filter response, iii) effects of post parameters on optimal filter design are made. These investigations have been utilized to estimate the values of radii for a particular dielectric constant and inter-post separation of posts used for design of broad band filter. Design and optimization of different parameters of dielectric posts has been done for a rectangular waveguide having 2x4 post configuration uniformly spaced and frequency dependent S parameters are computed for optimal BPF responses (discussed details are in chapter 3 of this thesis).

2.7.1.1 EFFECT OF POST RADIUS

One of the primary design parameters is the radius of the posts and proper range for the same is required to be chosen for application of the structure as BPF having broad VSWR BW and Band-Pass BW over a particular frequency band as per requirements. The ranges of radius of posts that can be used for fabrication of BPF with X band rectangular waveguide having 2x4 post configuration are restricted due to broad dimension of the waveguide, limitations are imposed on ranges of radius of posts useful for practical applications due to adequate mechanical support of post configuration and limitation to maintain exact spacing between two successive posts or two consecutive layers. Rectangular waveguide having 2x4 post configuration at X band is shown in Figure 2.12. Details of computation of range of post parameters for BPF response at X band are discussed here. The range of values of radius of post that can be used for design of BPF is shown in Table 2.3. The range of values of dielectric constant of post that can be used for design of BPF is shown in Table 2.4.

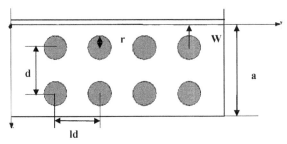

Figure 2.12 BPF configuration having 2x4 dielectric posts inside X band rectangular waveguide

(i)   Let a=broad dimension of waveguide, r=radius of posts, d= separation between centers of the posts, ld=interlayer separation.

(ii)   Considering *geometrical factors and mechanical fabrication* issues ranges of post radii that can be considered for design of BPF response using X band rectangular waveguide are (0.5-5.0) mm.

(iii)   Range of radii of posts that can be used to obtain BPF response from 2x4 post configuration inside rectangular waveguide structure are dependent on *EM scattering, dielectric constant of the posts, other design parameters* and is observed to be (1.5-4.2) mm. for X band.

(iv)   W (distance of centre of the post from waveguide wall) = 0.5*(a-d) or a=2*W+d .

(v)   Minimum distance of edges of dielectric posts from the waveguide wall required to support mechanical fabrication of the post structure inside waveguide is 1.0 mm and the same computed from centre of the posts used for design of BPF are r+1.0.

(vi)   Range of W is (6.8-10.0) mm. for ranges of radius of posts used to design the BPF configuration under consideration where EM scattering from posts is sufficient to form BPF response within X band.

(vii)   Considering mechanical fabrication minimum inter-post separation (3.0 mm) between two consecutive posts having radius 1.5 mm. (minimum value for BPF response) has been used to compute upper range of W as 10.0 mm. Similarly maximum value of inter-post separation (9.4 mm) between two consecutive posts having radius 4.2 mm (maximum value for BPF response) has been used to compute lower range of W as 6.8 mm.

Figure 2.13 shows nature of variation of VSWR BW and Band-Pass BW at X band for different radii of dielectric posts for 2x4 post configurations inside rectangular waveguide. The range of dielectric constant useful for filter response at X band using 2x4 post configuration inside rectangular waveguide is considered here to generate the plot. The filter structure having 2x4 post configuration inside rectangular waveguide is investigated for BPF response where dielectric constants of posts used to design the filter are varied within a small range along with the radii of the posts. Figure 2.14 shows nature of variation of VSWR BW and Band-Pass BW of the 2x4 post configuration inside rectangular waveguide (at X band) where radii of dielectric posts are varied to obtain the BPF response. The nature of variation of VSWR BW and Band-Pass BW of the BPF under consideration (at X band) where radii of dielectric posts are variable parameter for different inter-post distance used for design of the same as shown in Figure 2.15.

2.7.1.2 EFFECT OF POST MATERIAL

A parametric study is made to analyze the effect of post parameters on frequency dependent S parameters of the multi-post rectangular waveguide configuration and range of the permittivity of the post material useful for the synthesis of BPF response using X band waveguide is tabulated in Table 2.4. It is observed that formation of BPF response for a 2x4 post configuration inside X band rectangular waveguide is possible when dielectric constants of the posts are properly selected.

Figure 2.16 shows nature of variation of VSWR BW and Band-Pass BW of BPF at X band for different dielectric constant of posts and the range of radii useful for filter response at X band using 2x4 post configuration inside rectangular waveguide is considered here to generate the plot. The filter structure having 2x4 post configuration inside rectangular waveguide is investigated for BPF response where radii of dielectric posts used to design the same are varied within a small range along with the dielectric constant of the posts. Figure 2.17 shows nature of variation of VSWR BW and Band-Pass BW of the 2x4 post configuration inside rectangular waveguide (at X band) where dielectric constants of posts are varied to obtain the BPF response. The effects of dielectric constant of posts (used for design of waveguide filter) on VSWR BW and Band-Pass BW of BPF having 2x4 post configurations inside X band rectangular waveguide for variable inter-post separation is observed and shown in Figure 2.18. The effects of dielectric constant of posts (used for design of waveguide filter) on VSWR BW and Band-Pass BW of BPF at X band for 2x4 post configurations with variable inter-layer separation is observed and shown in Figure 2.19.

It is observed that the VSWR BW and Band-Pass BW of the BPF using 2x4 post configuration inside X band rectangular waveguide gradually decreases when the dielectric constant of the posts are increased. For a uniformly separated 2x4 post configuration inside X band rectangular waveguide VSWR BW and Band-Pass BW can be optimized when post parameters as radii and inter-post distance as well as interlayer separation are chosen according to the frequency of operation.

(viii)   Range of dielectric constant of posts used for obtaining BPF response using 2x4 post configurations inside rectangular waveguide are dependent on radius of the posts and other parameters and observed to be (6.0-85.0) for the structure under consideration within X band.

2.7.1.3 EFFECT OF INTER-POST SEPARATION

The effects of varying the post spacing on VSWR BW and Band-Pass BW for a small range of dielectric constants are investigated for a rectangular waveguide structure having 2x4 dielectric posts uniformly spaced as shown in Figure 2.20. For all other higher values of post spacing other than minimum VSWR BW and Band-Pass BW decreases and range of dielectric constants useful for obtaining BPF response at X band increases. The rectangular waveguide structure having 2x4 dielectric posts uniformly spaced are investigated for effects of post spacing on VSWR BW and Band-Pass BW for a small range of radii of dielectric posts as shown in Figure 2.21.

(ix)   Range of Inter-post separation/ interlayer spacing are computed as (9.4-12.6) mm. with the highest value of radius (4.2 mm.) of posts that can be used for BPF design at X band.

(x)   Range of Inter-post separation/ interlayer spacing is computed as (4.0-18.0) mm. for lowest value of radii (1.5 mm.) of posts that can be used for BPF design at X band

(xi)   The maximum permissible inter-post separation for design of BPF response is 12.6 mm. at X band. It is also observed that for optimum frequency responses in terms of VSWR BW and Band-Pass BW, radius of posts for design of BPF at X band is required to be maximum (within the range of fabrication) and inter-post separation needs to be minimum for the geometry under consideration. The effect of interlayer separation on VSWR BW and Band-Pass BW is also studied and it is observed that for interlayer separation required to be same as that of inter-post separation for optimum VSWR BW and Band-Pass BW irrespective of radii of posts used for BPF design.

(xii)   It is observed that range of dielectric constant useful for BPF response is higher when inter-post separation is more and the estimated VSWR BW and Band-Pass BW is less compared to that for lower values of inter-post separation.

These findings can be utilized for design of filter having broad VSWR BW and Band-Pass BW where choice of dielectric constant for a particular inter-post separation and radii of the posts can be made depending on requirement.

2.7.1.4 EFFECT OF INTERLAYER SPACING

Figure 2.22-2.24 shows the effect of interlayer separation of 2x4 post configurations inside X band rectangular waveguide on VSWR BW and Band-Pass BW of filter under consideration for variations of post parameters like dielectric constant, radii and inter-post separations. The effect of variation of inter-layer separation on VSWR BW and Band-Pass BW of a 2x4 posts configuration inside rectangular waveguide at X band is observed for a small range of dielectric constant of posts as shown in Figure 2.22.The effect of variation of inter-layer separation of dielectric posts on VSWR BW and Band-Pass BW of a 2x4 posts configuration inside rectangular waveguide at X band is observed to be non linear for variation of radii of posts as shown in Figure 2.23.The effect of inter-layer separation of dielectric posts on VSWR BW and Band-Pass BW of BPF structure under consideration is observed for different values of inter-post spacing and shown in Figure 2.24.

2.7.2 OBSERVATIONS ON EFFECTS OF POST PARAMETERS FOR DESIGN OF BPF

The structure having multiple dielectric posts uniformly spaced in multi-layer configurations inside rectangular waveguide has been studied to synthesis BPF response having broad VSWR BW and Band-Pass BW at particular frequency band. Trained ANN model of the rectangular waveguide structure having 2x4 post configuration is considered for computing the range of design parameters of the same for obtaining broadband BPF response at X band. The physical and positional parameter of the structure having multi-post multi-layer dielectric posts inside rectangular waveguide decides the nature of BPF responses in terms of frequency dependent S parameters.

Sometimes parameters of posts required for design of BPF are not physically realizable. An extensive study on useful range of post material and dimensions where BPF response having broad VSWR BW and Band-Pass BW is physically realizable is observed using uniformly arranged four layer (2x4) two post configurations inside rectangular waveguide at X band and can further be utilized for design of optimal BPF.

1.   It is observed that 2x4 configuration of dielectric posts arranged in a uniform manner inside rectangular waveguide is optimum in size, fabrication complexity and sufficient to study the nature of variation of VSWR BW and Band-Pass BW of the structure under consideration for different parameters of posts.

2.   It is observed that the variation of S_{21} with frequency for 2x4 post configuration inside X band rectangular waveguide is significant for higher dielectric constant and BPF response over X band is observed when dielectric constants of the posts are higher than a cutoff value.

3.   The effects of variations of radii of dielectric posts on VSWR BW and Band-Pass BW of BPF response from rectangular waveguide structure are observed. Nature of variation of VSWR BW and Band-Pass BW for change in dielectric constant of posts is steeper for higher value of radii.

4.   For a multilayer two post configuration where posts are uniformly separated inside X band rectangular waveguide it is observed that higher VSWR BW and Band-Pass BW can be obtained for posts having lower dielectric constants when suitable filter radii, inter-post distance as well as interlayer separation are chosen according to the frequency of operation. It is observed that radius of posts must be larger (within the fabrication limit), when lower dielectric constant are used for synthesis of BPF. Higher VSWR BW and Band-Pass BW can be obtained when posts having larger radii and lower dielectric constant are used.

5.   Filter pass-band shifts toward lower end when dielectric constant is increased and VSWR BW and Band-Pass BW depends on the post configuration as well as on the post parameters like dielectric constant, radii, inter-post separation etc. in a non linear way.

6.   It is further observed that for higher values of dielectric constant of the post material VSWR BW and Band-Pass BW decreases non-linearly and % changes of VSWR BW and Band-Pass BW for the BPF configuration under consideration is much less compared to that for lower values of dielectric constant of the post material.

7.   It is also observed that VSWR BW and Band-Pass BW of the configuration under study increases with increasing radii of posts when inter-post separation is decreased up to the permissible value decided by mechanical/geometrical factors.

8.   It is observed that posts having lowest dielectric constant and largest radii is most suitable for obtaining maximum VSWR BW and Band-Pass BW of the BPF structure under consideration. VSWR BW and Band-Pass BW is optimum for practically available posts having highest value of radii and lowest value of dielectric constant.

9.   To enhance the VSWR BW and Band-Pass BW more number of layers can be added and depending on the restriction on the physical size of the filter the number of layers of the BPF configuration can be selected.

10.   It is observed that the VSWR BW and Band-Pass of the filter having 2x4 post configurations inside X band rectangular waveguide is dependent on post separation and maximum for minimum separation between two consecutive posts practically achievable with the configuration under study.

11.   It is observed that VSWR BW and Band-Pass BW of BPF configuration under consideration increases with increasing radii of posts and decreases with increasing dielectric constant of posts. Maximum VSWR BW and Band-Pass BW of the filter configuration is possible when highest permissible radii of posts are used along with lowest permissible inter-post separation.

12.   It is also observed that the effect of dielectric constant is more significant for obtaining optimum BPF response of the filter structure under consideration compared to the effect of radii on the same.

13.   It is observed that effect of inter-post distance is more significant for obtaining optimum BPF response of the filter structure under consideration compared to the effect of radii on the same. It is observed that range of dielectric constant is minimum where lowest permissible inter-post separation is considered for design of BPF at X band.

14.   It is also observed that maximum VSWR BW and Band-Pass BW of the rectangular waveguide having 2x4 post configuration is possible when lowest permissible inter-post separation used for design of the BPF along with minimum inter-layer separation. For unequal values of inter-post separation and inter-layer separation VSWR BW and Band-Pass BW is always less than the optimum and it is observed that range of variation of VSWR BW and Band-Pass BW of BPF is higher where minimum permissible values of inter-post separation is used along with different inter-layer separations. This is in contrast with the case where minimum permissible values of inter-layer separation are used along with different inter-post separations. This can be explained as

i)   the post configuration is not symmetric,

ii)   more number of post layers are added,

iii)   VSWR BW of the filter configuration increases due to addition of each layer where minimum permissible values of inter-layer separation are used for the design and optimization of BPF under consideration.

15.   It has been observed that   i) Range of dielectric constant can be computed from trained ANN model of the filter configuration under consideration and BPF responses are generated within the X band due to scattering of EM waves from posts. VSWR BW and Band-Pass BW of the filter structure having 2x4 post configuration inside rectangular waveguide monotonically decreases over the range of dielectric constant.

16.   It has been found that ranges of values of radius of posts that can be used for practical fabrication of the BPF is different from the same as computed using trained ANN model. The reasons are due to constraint imposed on mechanical fabrication of the filter structure and are depended on accuracy of the tools used for same.

17.   It has been observed for waveguides having dimensions operating at higher frequency band the post radii required to synthesize BPF response are lower compared to that of X band. In addition to this the range of the dielectric constant of the posts that can be used for design of BPF is smaller.

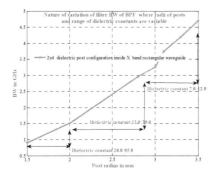

Figure 2.13 Effects of radius of dielectric posts on VSWR BW and Band-Pass BW of BPF for 2x4 post

configuration inside rectangular waveguide at X band

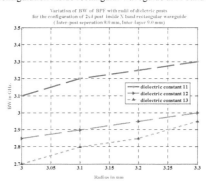

Figure 2.14 Variation of VSWR BW and Band-Pass BW (at X band) for variation of radius of posts used to

design the BPF (range of dielectric constants of posts are considered)

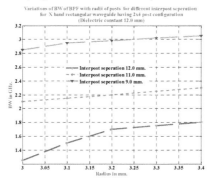

Figure 2.15 Variation of VSWR BW and Band-Pass BW of BPF (at X band) for variation of radius of posts

used to design the BPF (range of inter-post separations are considered)

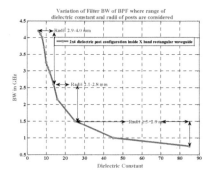

Figure 2.16 Nature of variation of VSWR BW and Band-Pass BW of the BPF where usable range of dielectric constant and radius of posts are considered for X band rectangular waveguide having 2x4 post configuration uniformly separated

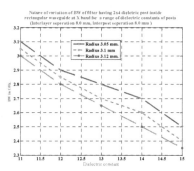

Figure 2.17 Effect of dielectric constant of posts on VSWR BW and Band-Pass BW of BPF for a small range of radii of posts

(Inter-layer/Inter-post separation 8.0 mm)

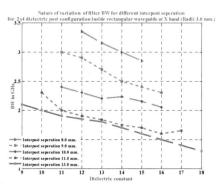

Figure 2.18 Effects of dielectric constant of posts on VSWR BW and Band-Pass BW of BPF for a range of inter-post separation (Radius of posts = 3.0 mm, Interlayer distance is same as inter post separation)

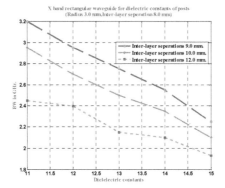

Figure 2.19 Effects of dielectric constant of posts on VSWR BW and Band-Pass BW of BPF for a range of inter-layer separation of post (Radius 3.0 mm, Inter-post separation 8.0 mm)

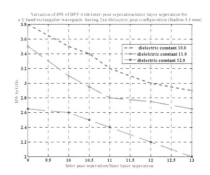

Figure 2.20 Effects of inter-post separation on VSWR BW and Band-Pass BW of BPF for a range of dielectric constant of posts (Radius of posts = 3.3 mm, Interlayer distance is same as that of inter post separation)

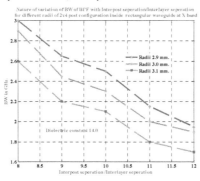

Figure 2.21 Effects of inter post separation on VSWR BW and Band-Pass BW of BPF for a range of radii of posts(Dielectric constant 14.0, Interlayer distance is same as that of inter post separation)

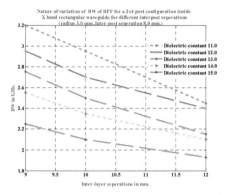

Figure 2.22 Effects of inter-layer separation of posts on VSWR BW and Band-Pass BW of BPF with variable dielectric constant of posts (Radius of posts is 3.0 mm, Inter-post separation is 8.0 mm)

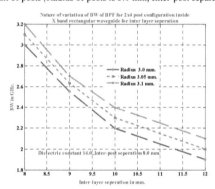

Figure 2.23 Effects of inter-layer separation of posts on VSWR BW and Band-Pass BW of BPF with variable radii of posts (Dielectric constant 14.0, Inter-post separation 8.0 mm)

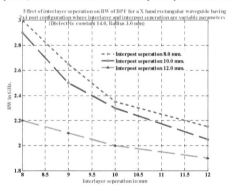

Figure 2.24 Effects of inter-layer separation on VSWR BW and Band-Pass BW of BPF for different inter-post separations (Radius of posts 3.0 mm, Dielectric constant 14.0 mm)

2.8 OPTIMAL DESIGN OF 2X4 POST WAVEGUIDE (UNIFORM) USING AI TECHNIQUE

In order to design multi-post multi-layer rectangular waveguide as BPF having desired S_{21} and S_{11}, design and optimization of different parameters of dielectric post configuration are required to be done. Here one rectangular waveguide (X band) structure having four layered two post configuration with uniform radii and uniform separation of posts has been considered for design of optimal BPF using selected parameters of dielectric posts(within the limit of mechanical fabrication)

The aim of this research is to use AI technique for design and optimization of design parameters of the filter structure having multiple dielectric posts inside rectangular waveguide. Here trained ANN model of rectangular waveguide having 2x4 dielectric posts configuration along with GA optimization techniques are used to optimize the transmittance/reflectance of the same. To enhance the applicability of the structure as BPF having broad VSWR and Band-Pass BW the BPF configuration under consideration has been optimized using ANN-GA technique. A suitable cost function is defined for the frequency band under consideration and used for optimization of BPF with proper weight ages of the parameters need to optimize. In these process particular values of radii and dielectric constants of posts selected by the optimization algorithm is further used to compute the frequency response of optimal BPF using EM simulation. The measured performance of the waveguide BPF under consideration is compared with that of simulated performance for verification of the methodology adapted. Here One rectangular waveguide BPF at X band is designed, optimized, fabricated and its measured frequency response performance of the same is compared with that of the simulated one (details are discussed in chapter 3).

Different aspects of design/optimization process are discussed in this chapter and chapter 3-5 contain applications of the AI techniques for optimal design of three different filter structures. Optimization techniques has been applied for optimization of VSWR and Band-Pass BW of one SSL filter and one microstrip ring filter where trained ANN model is used for development of optimal BPF within the frequency band under consideration (details are discussed in chapter 4-5).The utility of AI techniques and its applicability in place of EM simulator is justified using measurement results of developed BPF where experimental verification of optimized design are carried out and compared with those of the theoretical / simulation results. The work can be further extended for other filter structures and frequency bands.

2.9 BPF RESPONSE OF MULTI-POST MULTI-LAYERED WAVEGUIDE (NON UNIFORM)

Frequency response of rectangular waveguide structures having multiple dielectric posts in multilayer configuration where parameters of dielectric posts are varied in a non uniform manner has been studied here and included in this chapter. It is observed that instead of uniform separation and uniform radius, filter configurations having multiple dielectric posts inside rectangular waveguide using non uniform parameters like unequal radii of posts and inter post separation can be used to synthesize filter response and is useful for specialized applications. Here studies made on multi-post multi-layer rectangular waveguide structures having dielectric posts with non uniform parameters (radius or post separation) and it is observed that BPF/BSF responses over a frequency band can be obtained when suitable combination of parameters of posts are selected. Here the computations of frequency dependent S parameters are carried out in the same process as in the case of uniform array of posts inside rectangular waveguide. The responses of synthesized filters are computed using EM simulation and new finding are observed, interpreted and published in a book chapter by the author along with other co-authors [160].

Two different types of non uniform distribution of dielectric post configuration are chosen to design the filter and its frequency response characteristics is observed using EM simulation. The first choices of parameters are uniform separation between adjacent two-posts and non uniform radii of the posts subject to Chebyshev distribution. The period h of 8-layered two-posts (the separation distance along the waveguide axis between the adjacent post planes) is fixed as they satisfy the following relation $\beta(\omega_0) = \pi / h$ where β is the propagation constant of the TE_{10} mode and ω_0 is the center angular frequency for the rejection band. The value of ω_0 can be chosen to be within a particular frequency band and $\beta(\omega_0)$ and h is determined. The radii of the posts are changed proportional to the rate

$$
\begin{array}{c}
1^{st} \text{ layer, 2nd layer, } 3^{rd} \text{ layer, } 4^{th}, \quad 5^{th}, \quad 6^{th}, \quad 7^{th}, \quad 8^{th} \\
\hline
0.49, \quad 0.71, \quad 0.78, \quad 1.0, \quad 1.0, \quad 0.78, \quad 0.71, \quad 0.49
\end{array}
\tag{2.1}
$$

Second choice of parameters is a non uniform separation between the adjacent two-posts having non uniform radius of the posts subject to Gaussian distribution using the relation,

$$
\beta(\omega_0) = \pi / h_4, \quad h_4 = z_5 - z_4 \tag{2.2}
$$

h_4 along with $h_j (= z_{j+1} - z_j)$ are determined through the following equation

$$
h_{4+j} = h_4(1 + j\delta)\,(j = 0, \pm 1, \pm 2, \pm 3) \tag{2.3}
$$

where δ is a parameter for chirping ($\delta = 0.05$ is taken). The radii R_i of the posts are changed as

$$
R_i = R_{max}\, e^{-2(d_i / L)^2} \tag{2.4}
$$

where $R_4 = R_5 = R_{max}$, $L = z_8 - z_1$, and $d_i = |z_i - (z_4 + z_5)/2|$ indicate the distance from the center of the layered structure to the i-th pair of two posts.

In Figure 2.25 3D view of waveguide filter having dual dielectric posts in 2x8 configurations with uniform radius and spacing is shown. For the case of 2x8 post configuration having uniform radii and separation inside rectangular waveguide structure at X band, frequency depended S parameters are computed and shown in Figure 2.26.

51

(i)

Figure 2.25 Rectangular waveguide filter having dual dielectric posts in 2x8 configurations with uniform radius and spacing

Filter configuration having 2x8 dielectric posts inside X band rectangular waveguide with non uniform radius and uniform separation of the post layers according to Chebyshev distribution is shown in Figure 2.27. Here radii of posts are variable according to Chebyshev distribution and other parameters of the configuration are set as inter layer separation = 10.0 mm., ε_r = 12.5, inter post separation = 10.0 mm. The BPF response is computed using EM simulation and is observed as 8.15-11.3 GHz for this configuration as shown in Figure 2.28.

The waveguide structures having 16 dielectric posts in 2x8 configuration with non-uniform parameters of posts is considered here for study and is shown in Figures 2.27-2.28. In the case of non uniform distribution of geometrical parameters of posts where radius and spacing follows a predefined amplitude distribution (as Chebyshev or Gaussian) the frequency depended scattering reflectance and transmittance are computed using EM simulation and results are shown in Figures 2.29-2.30.

Filter configuration having 2x8 dielectric posts inside X band rectangular waveguide with non uniform radius and non uniform separation of the post layers according to Gaussian distribution is shown in Figure 2.29. Here radii of posts are variable, inter-layer separation varies according to Gaussian distribution and other parameters of the post configuration under study are inter-post separation = 9.0 mm., ε_r = 10.5. The BPF response is computed using EM simulation and is observed as 10.0 -11.75 GHz for this configuration as shown in Figure 2.30.

TABLE 2.1 Accuracy of developed ANN model

Post configuration /Average error	Training		Testing	
	$\lvert S_{11}\rvert$	$\lvert S_{21}\rvert$	$\lvert S_{11}\rvert$	$\lvert S_{21}\rvert$
Single conducting post	.001	.01	0.08	0.04
Single dielectric post	0.1	0.05	0.2	0.08
Eight(2x4) dielectric post	0.1	0.05	0.2	0.07

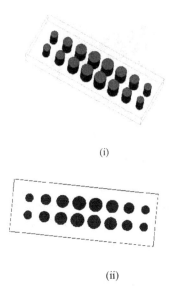

(i)

(ii)

Figure 2.26 Rectangular waveguide filter having sixteen dielectric posts in 2x8 configurations with uniform spacing and non uniform radius according to Chebyshev distribution ,(i) 3D view, (ii) 2D view

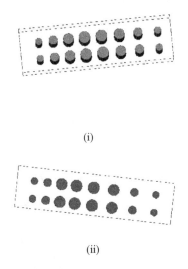

(i)

(ii)

Figure 2.27 Rectangular waveguide filter having sixteen dielectric posts in 2x8 configurations with non uniform spacing and non uniform radius according to Gaussian distribution, (i) 3D view, (ii) 2D view

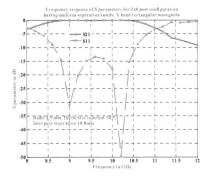

Figure 2.28 Frequency responses of S parameters for 2x8 post configuration having uniform radii and inter-post separation inside X band rectangular waveguide

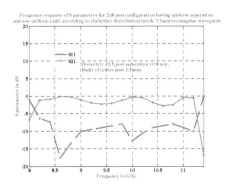

Figure 2.29 Frequency responses of S parameters for 2x8 post configuration inside X band rectangular waveguide having uniform radii and non uniform inter-layer separation according to Chebyshev distribution

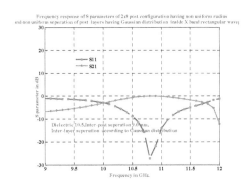

Figure 2.30 Frequency responses of S parameters for 2x8 post configuration inside X band rectangular waveguide having non uniform radii and non uniform inter-layer separation according to Gaussian distribution

TABLE 2.2 Ranges of parameters of dielectric posts for multi-layer multi-post rectangular waveguide filter at X band

Parameter	Computed Values
Post radius(r)	1.5-4.2 mm.
W (distance of centre of the post from waveguide wall)	6.8-10.0 mm.
Inter-post separation (d)	4.0-18.0 mm. (post radii 1.5 mm) 9.4-12.6 mm. (post radii 4.2 mm)
Dielectric constant	6.0-85.0

Table 2.3 Effects of dielectric constant on BPF response (2x4 posts)

(Range of radii of dielectric posts for design of BPF at X band)

(Inter-post separation = 9.0 mm. and interlayer separation= 9.0 mm)

Dielectric constants of posts in 2x4 configuration	Lower and upper cutoff values of radii for design of BPF response at X band (mm.)	Range of radii for design of BPF response at X band (mm.)	Maximum VSWR BW in GHz.
6.0	4.18-4.2	0.02	4.2
7.0	3.99-4.02	0.03	4.1
8.0	3.8-3.84	0.04	4.0
9.0	3.52-3.7	0.18	3.7
10.0	3.3-3.56	0.26	3.25
11.0	3.16-3.5	0.34	3.1
12.0	2.9-3.34	0.44	2.95
14.0	2.65-3.2	0.55	2.6
16	2.45-3.05	0.6	2.15
25	1.9-2.6	0.7	1.5
45	1.7-2.6	0.9	1.0
85	1.5-2.7	1.2	0.75

Table 2.4 Effects of radii of dielectric posts on BPF response (2x4 posts)

(Range of dielectric constant of posts for design of BPF at X band)

(Inter-post separation = 9.0 mm. and interlayer separation= 9.0 mm)

Radii of dielectric posts in mm.	Lower and upper cutoff values of dielectric constant for BPF response at X band	Range of dielectric constant for BPF response at X band (mm.)	Maximum VSWR BW in GHz.
3.5	7.0-10.0	3.0	4.7
3.3	8.0-12.0	4.0	4.2
3.1	9.0-13.0	5.0	3.75
3.0	10.0-16.0	6.0	3.25
2.8	12.0-20.0	8.0	2.95
2.0	20.0-40.0	20.0	1.5
1.5	40.0-85.0	45.0	0.9

2.10 DISCUSSIONS

It is observed the range of parameters that can be used for design of BPF using rectangular waveguide structure having 2x4 post configuration is constrained by mechanical and geometrical factors and has to be considered before selection of the same. It is also observed that practical limitations on fabrication accuracies plays major role in achieving desired results as per design/simulation. In practical design parameters of BPF may differ from those values predicted by the optimization algorithm and depending on practical resources parameters of posts used to develop/fabricate the BPF may not be same as that of design/optimized values.

In practice neither the available fabrication accuracies support the design/optimized values of positional parameters of dielectric posts, nor the design/optimized values of radius or dielectric constant of dielectric posts as predicted by the optimization algorithm used for design of the filter configuration under consideration. It may happen that the predicted parameters of the post as per optimal design of BPF may differ significantly from practically available parameters of posts. Hence depending on the final fabrication process frequency response of the BPF will be different from that estimated by the optimization algorithm.

2.11 SUMMARY

Theoretical analysis and parametric study using AI techniques are made on multi-post multi-layer rectangular waveguide structure. Frequency responses of the BPF configuration under considerations are computed in terms of frequency dependent S parameters and included in this chapter. Further design and optimization of band-pass/band-stop responses using rectangular waveguide structure having dielectric post configuration can be done using soft computing techniques. Theoretical formulations using MATLAB code are used to compute data for development of a trained ANN model of uniformly spaced equii-radii dielectric post (2x4) configuration inside rectangular waveguide structure at X band. Based on those trained ANN models of multi-post multi-layer rectangular waveguide the frequency response of scattering reflectance and transmittance of the same are studied in detail. Different sets of post parameters of the BPF structure under consideration are computed from its trained ANN model and frequency dependent reflectance and transmittance of multi-post multi-layer rectangular waveguide structures are computed. The range of post parameters useful for synthesis of BPF response using the same are also computed for X band and included in this chapter. These studies are also used to synthesize BPF and BSF characteristics from multi-post multi-layer waveguide structure involving non-uniform radii and separation of dielectric posts. This proposed design technique for the BPF configuration having multi-post multi-layer structure inside rectangular waveguide can be further extended for other frequency bands and the proposed modeling and optimization technique can be generalized for other practical problems.

3

OPTIMAL DESIGN OF A WAVEGUIDE BPF USING ANN-GA TECHNIQUE

3.1 INTRODUCTION

The aim of the research work (part of this thesis) is to design and optimize waveguide filters using AI techniques [128-135]. Here an X band rectangular waveguide having eight dielectric posts arranged symmetrically in four layer configuration with two posts per layer is considered. Figure 3.1-3.2 shows 3D and 2D views of the waveguide filter configuration under consideration.

Figure 3.1 3D view of waveguide filter model with eight posts in 2x4 configurations

To formulate EM scattering from multiple dielectric posts inside rectangular waveguide structure image theory is utilized for derivation of mathematical expressions for frequency dependent S parameters of the same. Theoretical analysis of scattering from multi-post multi-layer rectangular waveguide utilizing concept of image theory, Lattice Sum and T-matrix are carried out to compute frequency dependent transmission and reflection coefficients of S parameters of the structure. Mathematical expressions for reflection and transmission matrices of

(i)   Rectangular waveguide structure having single post (conducting/dielectric),

(ii)   1x2 dielectric post configuration periodically arranged inside rectangular waveguide and

(iii)   Generalized expressions for multiple posts in multilayer configuration inside rectangular waveguide are included in Appendix of this thesis.

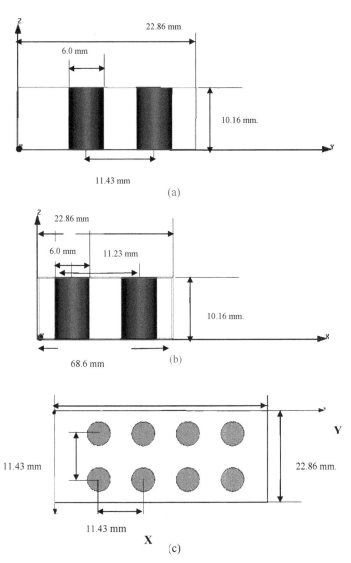

Figure 3.2 2D view of waveguide filter having eight posts in four layer configuration (a) YZ plane (b) XZ plane (c) XY plane

Detailed theoretical expressions and mathematical steps for analysis of the structure are discussed in literatures [155-158]. MATLAB code has been used to compute the generalized frequency response of S parameters of the structures under consideration at X band and can be used further for similar structure at other frequency bands. In order to use the AI technique for development of an optimal filter an ANN model of the rectangular waveguide structures having 2x4 dielectric post configurations

58

is considered. An ANN model of the structure under consideration produces frequency responses of S parameters of the same over the desired frequency range when it is trained and tested using the data generated from the scattering analysis. It is observed that results obtained using AI techniques are reasonably accurate compared to that obtained from EM simulator for design and optimization of the structure under consideration. Here basic research has been initiated to establish the fact that this methodology is useful and can be a suitable replacement of optimization procedure using EM simulator that needs costly infrastructure.

3.2 ANN-GA MODEL OF 2X4 POSTS INSIDE RECTANGULAR WAVEGUIDE

The frequency depended S matrices of a rectangular waveguide having multiple dielectric posts in multilayer configuration are computed using expressions included in Appendix. Data for frequency dependent S parameters are generated from the mathematical computations using MATLAB using the expression included in Appendix and is utilized to train the ANN model of a rectangular waveguide at X band having eight dielectric posts uniformly separated in four layer configuration where each layer is having two posts as shown in Figure 3.1-3.2.

The effects of design parameters of multi-post multi-layer rectangular waveguide configuration on reflectance and transmittance of the same are studied in detail and are included in chapter 2. The ranges of parameters taken for the design of ANN model of the rectangular waveguide structure having 2x4 dielectric posts are tabulated in Table 3.1.The ANN model has been trained using 450 data (computed from scattering analysis as stated in Appendix) of frequency depended S parameters of 2x4 dielectric post configuration at X band. The training accuracy of $|S_{11}|$ is set at 0.1 and that of $|S_{21}|$ is 0.05. The accuracy of ANN model is validated using 250 testing data of frequency depended S parameters for 2x4 dielectric post configuration at X band as computed from scattering analysis (Appendix) that are not used for testing purpose. The accuracy of the developed ANN model is shown in Table 3.2.

It is observed that the structure can work as BPF when suitable combinations of post parameters are chosen in the frequency band of interest. The range of parameters of dielectric posts like radii, dielectric constants, inter-post separations, inter-layer separations are computed using trained and tested ANN model of the structure having 2x4 dielectric post configuration inside X band rectangular waveguide. The frequency dependent S-parameters and VSWR BW and Band-Pass BW of the structure are computed and studied for their suitability as BPF over the X band.

The effect of physical dimensions of waveguide, positions of dielectric posts like inter-post separations, interlayer separations, effect of design parameters of posts (radii, dielectric constant) are studied here for design of optimal BPF. In the process of optimization the physical parameters of posts, specifically dimension of the posts and their relative positions are altered using GA algorithm in order to get the maximum transmittance and minimum reflectance of the BPF under consideration over X band.

The values of post parameters required for optimum performance of the BPF structures under consideration are computed from ANN-GA algorithm. Details of the GA parameters chosen and applied for this problem are shown in Table 3.3. Cost function as shown in Equation 3.1 is used for optimization of transmittance and reflectance of the structure having 2x4 post configuration inside X band rectangular waveguide.

The output of the trained ANN model is used as input of the GA optimizer in order to maximize the transmittance and minimize the reflectance of the structure under consideration. The ANN-GA algorithm is used for optimum performance of rectangular waveguide structure having 2x4 dielectric posts designed to work as BPF. As a result of this optimization process, the physical dimensions and relative positions of the array of posts inside the waveguide structure under consideration are altered.

The frequency dependent scattering reflectance and transmittance of the waveguide structure under consideration are computed from ANN-GA algorithm and are used to compute the VSWR BW and Band-Pass BW of the optimal BPF. HFSS is used to compute the frequency response of $|S_{11}|$ and $|S_{21}|$ parameters of the BPF having eight dielectric posts in four layer configuration inside an X band rectangular waveguide. The simulated frequency response of $|S_{11}|$ and $|S_{21}|$ parameters of the BPF under consideration where optimized values of posts parameters obtained from the ANN-GA model of the same are used to compare the measured frequency response of $|S_{11}|$ and $|S_{21}|$ parameters of the BPF under consideration.

The technical details of filter design, procedure of optimization, fabrication and characterization of BPF are discussed in this chapter of the thesis. Details of filter measurement and verification process are also discussed and included in this chapter.

3.3 GA OPTIMIZATION

The cost function used in GA optimizer to optimize scattering reflectance and transmittance for a rectangular waveguide having 2x4 post configurations is

$$\text{Maximize F (i)} = \sum_i (W_1 S_{21} + W_2 / S_{22}) \qquad (3.1)$$

where $W_1 = W_2 = 0.5$ has been chosen here as weight parameters of the cost function and 80 frequency points within the frequency band from 8.0-12.0 GHz are taken for this optimization process using GA. The physical parameter like dielectric constant of the posts, diameter of the posts, post positions from waveguide axes are normalized with respect to their maximum permissible values and used as input for the ANN - GA model. The desired centre frequency of the filter is arithmetic mean of two band edge frequencies (8.0 GHz., 12.0 GHz.) which is 10.0 GHz. The parameters required to be modified for optimal design of the filter configuration under consideration as computed from trained ANN model of the 2x4 post rectangular waveguide structure and are used as input of the GA optimizer. Adequate numbers of points are required to run the GA optimizer repetitively in order to reach the global minima of the cost function used here.

GA optimizer and ANN model of the rectangular waveguide having eight posts in four layer configuration is utilized to minimize $|S_{21}|$ and maximize $|S_{11}|$ over X band. Values of the post parameters of the optimized waveguide filter using its trained/tested ANN model along with GA optimizer are tabulated in Table 3.4 and used to compute frequency dependent transmittance/reflectance of the optimal BPF as shown in Figure 3.3.

3.4 GA CONVERGENCE

In order to get maximum transmittance and minimum reflectance of the filter structure under concern roulette wheel selection technique is chosen where each individual gene is given a chance to become a parent in proportion to its fitness. GA's performance and its parameter setting depend on the function being solved. A parametric study is performed with three parameters like population size N, crossover probability and mutation probability and these parameters are chosen to have largest fitness value of the cost function as shown in Equation 3.1.

TABLE 3.1 Range of Input parameters used for ANN - GA model of multi-post rectangular waveguide at X band

Parameters	Range
Dielectric constant of the post	5.0-20.0
Dielectric post diameter	3.0-8.0 mm
Post spacing between two successive post (along X)	4.0-11.5 mm
Post spacing between two successive layers	4.0-11.5 mm
Number of Posts	02-12

3.5 OPTIMIZED FREQUENCY RESPONSE (ANN-GA MODEL) OF WAVEGUIDE BPF

The ANN model of filter structure using X band rectangular waveguide having eight dielectric posts in four layer two post configuration is optimized using GA with suitable cost function for maximum R.L. and minimum I.L. Values of post parameters for optimum frequency response of the BPF under consideration have been computed using ANN-GA model of the same. The dimensions of post parameters obtained from optimized design of the BPF under consideration using ANN - GA model of the same are shown in Table 3.4. The parameters of dielectric posts are computed from optimal design of waveguide filter (ANN-GA algorithm) and used to simulate frequency dependent transmittance and reflectance of the same using HFSS as shown in Figure 3.3. The frequency responses of S parameters of the optimized design of the BPF configuration under consideration are observed and tabulated in Table 3.5. It is observed that values of post parameters for optimum filter BW as obtained from ANN-GA model of the structure under consideration are not available from local resources. Using available resources parameters of the posts nearest to the required values for optimal design of the BPF under consideration are selected and are used for fabrication of the same as listed in Table 3.4. The frequency dependent transmittance and reflectance of the waveguide filter using the non-optimum parameters of dielectric posts are also computed using HFSS and is shown in Figure 3.4.

TABLE 3.2 Accuracy of developed ANN model of 2x4 post waveguide BPF

Average error	Training	Testing
$|S_{11}|$	0.1	0.2
$|S_{21}|$	0.05	0.07

Table 3.3 Selections of GA parameter

Operator	Type
Encoding	Binary
Population size	1024
Crossover	Double point
Crossover probability	0.5
Mutation	Bit inversion
Mutation Probability	0.05
Selection	Roulette wheel selection
Algorithm	Binary
Standard Deviation	0.01

TABLE 3.4 Post parameters used for design of BPF using WR-28

Parameters	Optimized Value (ANN-GA model)	Values used for fabrication
Dielectric post diameter	6.6 mm	6.0 mm
Dielectric post height	10.16 mm	10.16 mm
Dielectric constant of post	9.0	10.2
Inter-post distance	9.0 mm	9.0 mm
Inter-layer distance	9.0 mm	9.0 mm

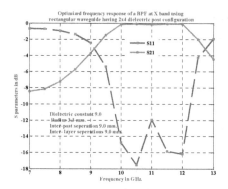

Figure 3.3 Frequency responses of S parameters of optimal waveguide filter (EM simulation)

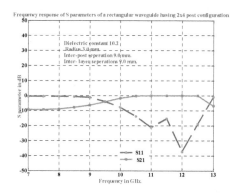

Figure 3.4 Simulated frequency response of S parameters of the waveguide filter (post parameters used for design of the same are listed in Table 3.4)

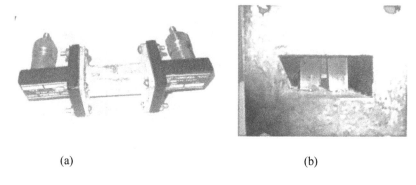

| (a) | (b) |

Figure 3.5 Fabricated waveguide filter (a) Assembled view (b) 2D view (XZ plane)

The optimized Band-Pass BW of the waveguide filter is 8.5-13.0 GHz with a S_{11} better than -5.0 dB over X band (ANN-GA model) and simulated Band-Pass BW of the same using non-optimum dimensions of dielectric posts is 9.4-12.8 GHz with S_{11} better than -5.0 dB over X band. The optimized VSWR BW of the waveguide filter is 9.3-12.5 GHz with a S_{11} better than -5.0 dB over X band (ANN-GA model) and simulated VSWR BW of the same using non-optimum dimensions of dielectric posts is 9.6-12.8 GHz with S_{11} better than -5.0 dB over X band.

Finally the filter is fabricated using X band rectangular waveguide and dielectric posts having parameters practically available (as shown in Table 3.4).After characterization using VNA (8720C) measured frequency response of the waveguide filter is compared with that of the simulated response and tabulated in Table 3.5.

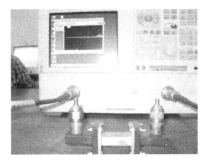

Figure 3.6 Measurement setup of the waveguide filter

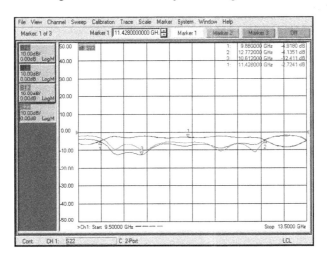

Figure 3.7 Measured frequency responses in terms of S_{21} and S_{11} of waveguide filter

3.6 FABRICATION OF THE WAVEGUIDE BPF

The layout of the BPF under consideration having dimensions as per Table 3.4 is drawn using AutoCAD (a drawing software tool) and fabrication of the same is done using CNC milling. The accuracy of CNC machining primarily depends on max rpm of the same. With 24000 rpm milling machine accuracy of 10 micrometer can be achieved. For the fabrication of waveguide having dielectric post configuration, mechanical factors like machine bed stability, referencing using laser probe, quality of cutting tools, along with CNC programming are few factors responsible for accuracy involved in fabrication related issues. The milling accuracy of CNC machine used here is 0.5mm and required accuracy is 0.1mm.

Here Aluminum (Al) sheet having thickness 0.8 mm is used for the fabrication of rectangular waveguide and flanges (required for connecting external connector or adaptor). Eight equal radii dielectric rods are used as posts which are placed inside the rectangular waveguide. For exact placement of the posts small grooves are made on top and bottom walls of the waveguide under consideration. This is required essentially to support mechanically the series of posts inside waveguide. The height of the posts are taken as the waveguide height minus the metal thickness of its wall to ensure proper fitting of the same and top surface of the posts needs to be flushed with the inside top surface of the waveguide walls. Practically the heights of the posts are taken slightly more than actually required in order to fit them tightly inside the grooves made for them. This in turn creates additional support for the series of posts and maintains uniform separation between them which is also an essential requirement for the design of the BPF.

TABLE 3.5 Comparison of simulated and measured performance of waveguide BPF

Filter Parameter	Simulated (eight post), Radius=3.3, Die constant=9.0,post separation =9.0 mm.	Simulated (eight post) Radius=3.0 mm, Die constant=10.2., post separation = 9.0 mm	Measured (eight post) Radius=3.0 mm, Die constant=10.2, post separation = 9.0 mm
VSWR BW(-5.0 dB)	9.3-12.5 = 3.2 GHz	9.6-12.8 = 3.2 GHz.	9.9-12.8 =2.9 GHz
Band-Pass BW (-5.0 dB)	8.5-13.0 = 4.5 GHz.	9.4-12.8 = 3.4 GHz.	9.9-12.8 =2.9 GHz

The dimensional accuracy as well as positional accuracy of the posts inside the waveguide is essential for mechanical point of view. Accuracy of the mechanical placement of dielectric posts in both lateral and longitudinal direction is required to obtain the desired frequency response of the S parameters of the optimum waveguide filter. The interaction of E field with the scattering amplitude of the 2x4 dielectric posts inside rectangular at X band depends on the geometrical positions of the posts under consideration. In addition to the choice of material parameters of the same, precautions are required for alignments as well as uniformity of the posts used for fabrication of the filter. A small trial and error process is adopted to fabricate the filter with practically achievable perfection in the mechanical fabrication process. The frequency dependent reflection and transmission characteristics of the BPF in terms of S parameters are observed to be deviating from its performance predicted by EM simulator using same set of design parameters. This discrepancy can be explained by the facts that fabrication limitations create inaccuracies in the position of the posts, their relative gap and alignment which are difficult to measure. Again accurate modeling of thin air gap at metal-dielectric junction is required in order to quantify this imperfection. The possible sources of error in fabrication/alignment process are discussed in section 3.8 of this thesis.

3.7 CHARACTERIZATION OF THE WAVEGUIDE BPF

The fabricated filter as shown in Figure 3.5(a) is integrated with suitable adaptor and the frequency response of S_{21} and S_{11} of this filter (reflection and transmission characteristics) in terms are measured using VNA (8720C) over X band. Measurement setup using VNA shown in Figure 3.6 is used to evaluate the frequency response of S_{21} and S_{11} for the fabricated waveguide filter. Table 3.5 shows a comparison of measured VSWR BW, Band-Pass BW, transmission and reflection coefficient of the fabricated BPF with that of the simulated one to assess quantitative performance of the same. Measured frequency response of S_{21} and S_{11} of the fabricated filter over X band are shown in Figure 3.7. It is observed that

The measured frequency response of S_{21} and S_{11} of the filter under consideration is BP in nature and observed to be 9.9 GHz to 12.8 GHz. Criterion used for computation of VSWR BW of the fabricated waveguide filter are set as the range of frequencies having $|S_{11}| < $ -5.0 dB and that for Band-Pass BW of the fabricated waveguide filter are set as the range of frequencies having $|S_{21}| > $ -5.0 dB.

i)   More than 26.0% fractional bandwidth (FBW) having centre frequency at 11.2 GHz is achieved in the X band with an insertion loss better than 3.0 dB.

ii)   The return loss is higher than expected due to reasons originated from mechanical point like fabrication inaccuracies, proper alignments and difficulty in maintaining exact spacing of posts inside the waveguide.

iii)   Manual and mechanical adjustments have been done for maximum possible accuracy of fabrication, but the available infrastructure does not support the requirements of fabrication accuracies to achieve the design parameters and hence desired frequency response of this filter could not be achieved.

66

iv)   The simulated frequency response of S parameters of the waveguide BPF as shown in Figure 3.4 is compared with that of the measured performance of the fabricated one as in Figure 3.7. The shift in the upper/lower and centre frequencies of optimal BPF response as shown in Figure 3.3 has been compared with that of the measured frequency responses. The reasons are due to use of non-optimum physical parameters of dielectric posts and lack of fabrication accuracies as well.

v)   The radii and dielectric constants of the posts used for fabrication are different compared to that required for design of optimal BPF as computed using ANN-GA model.

vi)   The measured result shows a BPF response from 9.9 GHz -12.8 GHz with an average return loss of 3.0 dB within the band. Experimentally verification of frequency response of X band rectangular waveguide has been done and is found to be working upto12.8 GHz.

vii)   Frequency response of the BPF in terms of scattering reflectance and transmittance can further be improved using better fabrication where small trial and error procedure can be adopted to correct the fabrication errors as much as possible.

viii)   Diameter of dielectric posts and their relative positions should be accurate enough to form the desired filter response within the frequency band of interest. There is no way to crosscheck the precision of parameters of fabricated filter like position of posts, relative placement, gaps between them and inter-post/inter-layer spacing etc with existing measurement facilities. The picture of side view of the fabricated filter is shown in Figure 3.5 (b) to explain these facts and higher precision in fabrication is required to obtain optimum VSWR BW and Band-Pass BW of S_{21} and S_{11} parameters for the BPF structure under consideration.

3.8 DISCREPANCIES IN FABRICATION PROCESS OF WAVEGUIDE BPF

In order to use the fabricated filter in any practical system fabrication of the filter need to be accurate enough to reproduce the simulated result within acceptable tolerance. Fabrication accuracies are required to be within acceptable tolerance and the design parameters of the optimal filter as computed from its ANN-GA model are required to be used for fabrication of the same.

The machining facilities at university workshops in India are generally not concerned about fabrication accuracies involved in the end product as they are not generating any revenue using their setup. For a PhD. student it becomes difficult to access the resources for accurate fabrication and professional fabrication facilities at places in India/abroad and it is difficult to bear the cost involved for fabrication. Also the long time frame for fabrication process for a single unit limits the possibility for repeated fabrication.

The machining facilities at university workshops has been utilized for fabrication of the filter and it has been seen that the dielectric posts are tilted with respect to each other and accuracy of their placements with respect to their relative positions are not possible to be checked after fabrication. It

67

can be estimated that 40% design efforts are lost in the fabrication process due to lack of accurate fabrication.

3.9 DISCUSSION

The fabrication process of the waveguide filter involves complicated mechanical steps. It is very difficult to measure fabrication inaccuracies like the position of the posts, their relative gap and alignment. Again insertion of dielectric rod inside hollow waveguide some thin air gap at metal-dielectric junction is created and accurate modeling is required in order to model this imperfection. This is reflected in the final frequency response as a loss term in reflectance and transmittance. It can be minimized using conducting glue at the air dielectric interface and characterizing the effect of the glue on overall performance of the filter. Higher I.L. due to inaccuracy of mechanical fabrication of the filter can be improved with better fabrication facilities, correction techniques, using precautions before and after fabrication and proper pre measurement steps.

Frequency response performance of the filter can be further improved when more number of filter sections are used which in turn increase cost and weight of the filter which is undesirable. The verification of the frequency response performance can be extended for other frequency bands (higher or lower) where the ANN model is required to be trained and optimization of the filter using GA has to be carried out for a different frequency band.

Here basic research has been performed to validate the design and optimization procedure of the filter under consideration using AI techniques and not to use the BPF for commercial and user required applications. The usefulness of the ANN-GA modeling technique in microwave filter design and optimization is illustrated practically in this chapter and can be used for design optimization of other filters having different specifications in microwave frequency ranges.

3.10 SUMMARY

In this chapter, the trained ANN model of eight dielectric posts in four layer configuration inside X band rectangular waveguide is used to design BPF and is utilized for optimization of bandwidth of the filter using GA. It is observed that the structure can work as BPF when parameters of dielectric post are chosen in the frequency band of interest. This type of model is very useful in optimization problems to predict frequency response of S parameters without using EM simulation. A trained and tested ANN model of the BPF under consideration produces frequency responses of S parameters of the same over a frequency band. This model is also useful for performing repetitive work where accuracies of output parameters depend on complexities of ANN model. Here basic research has been initiated to establish the fact that this methodology is useful and can be a suitable replacement of EM simulation process that needs costly infrastructure. Regarding accuracies of results produces by ANN model and those by EM simulation the former is acceptable for all research purposes and later is required for all user oriented projects where some predefined target specifications are required to be met by the designer and no relaxation may be allowed in the same. The accuracy of the trained ANN model is dependent on frequency range over it is trained for but response of the model is much faster compared to EM simulators. This is mainly due to the approximation involved in the ANN model and higher complexity of EM simulator.

The basic aim of this research work is to find new innovative process for filter design and efficient modeling. ANN-GA modeling is chosen for design of multi-post multi-layer filter using rectangular waveguide at X band and fabricated filter is characterized for verification of the usefulness of the chosen modeling technique. Repeated measurements have been made to verify the measured results with that of the simulated design. The desired result deviates from measured result due to several reasons but for fundamental research this is a stepping stone to establish the role and usefulness of ANN-GA modeling technique in microwave filter design and optimization. In addition to this work other two other filters has been designed and modeled using Artificial Intelligence techniques. Fabrication and subsequent measured results are included in this thesis to illustrate the usefulness of these techniques in filter design and optimization process.

4

OPTIMAL DESIGN OF A SUSPENDED STRIP LINE (SSL) FILTER USING ANN-GA TECHNIQUE

4.1 INTRODUCTION

Here research work has been carried out to design and optimize a BPF using Suspended Strip Line (SSL) structure having multiple broadside-offset coupled strip resonators. A strong coupling structure is incorporated in the proposed design to obtain wide VSWR BW and Band-Pass BW in the K to Ka frequency band (18.0-40.0 GHz.). The design parameters of the filter structure, SSL channel under consideration are modified using GA for optimization of VSWR BW and Band-Pass BW of the same and ANN-GA model of the SSL BPF has been developed. In this process design parameters of the filter structure under consideration are modified and optimized frequency response of reflectance and transmittance of the same are computed, simulated and compared with the measured frequency response of the fabricated BPF to validate the usefulness of the design/optimization procedure.

In this chapter, a fifteen section BPF in SSL configuration is designed and synthesized in edge coupled configuration with broadside-offset coupled resonator elements. The utility of AI techniques for design and optimization of SSL filter are reflected when the frequency dependent reflectance and transmittance of the same are measured and compared with that of optimal design computed using its ANN-GA model.

4.2 SSL FILTER CONFIGURATION

SSL is a transmission medium with moderate loss suitable for applications in the upper microwave and lower millimeter-wave frequency ranges [5,10]. Using this technology design and development of both broadband and narrowband filters in HP, LP, BP, BS configurations are reported [88-90]. SSL structure shown in Figure 4.1(a) has one dielectric substrate suspended symmetrically between two ground planes within a shielded cavity and conducting metal strip printed on both sides of the dielectric substrate [83,116-123]. The artwork of the filter as per design can be transferred on metal strips of the SSL configuration by using suitable fabrication process.

The attractive features of SSL compared to conventional stripline or microstrip are reduced ohmic / dielectric losses over wide bandwidth, better temperature stability over a wide temperature range, low dispersion and good fabrication tolerances. The SSL structure can be used for synthesis of broadband filter with broadside coupled resonator printed on a substrate suspended in a shielded channel. The BPF having SSL structure uses quarter wavelength resonators and the capacitive coupling is realized through the supporting dielectric, eliminating the need for precision etching. Suspended substrate strip line is very low loss and useful for design of broad band filters and multiplexers which can be fed with coaxial cable or conventional waveguide.

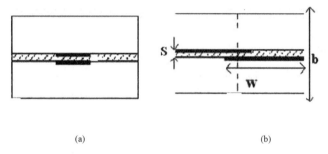

(a)   (b)

Figure 4.1: Cross-section of the suspended strip-line configuration in

(a) broad-side coupled strips (b) broadside-offset coupled strips

S = substrate height, b = height of SSL channel, W = width of strip elements

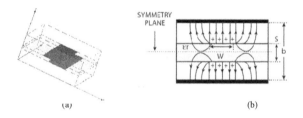

(a)   (b)

Figure 4.2 (a) 3D view of broadside offset coupled suspended strip-line resonator (b) Field configuration of TEM

4.3 DESIGN OF SSL FILTER

First step of this design process is to study the effects of design parameters on the filter performance. To implement theoretical design practically the effects of design parameters need to be considered to realize the design within the accuracy level of fabrication errors.

Here broadside offset coupled strips in edge coupled configuration have been chosen as resonators and realized using SSL structure [73-83]. Broadside-coupled suspended substrate resonators are

71

basically an arrangement of conducting strip elements on both sides of the substrate in an unsymmetrical configuration with an offset between the strips for improved coupling between resonators as shown in Figure 4.1. Here investigation has been made to design, develop and optimize the BPF as per some tentative specifications.

BPF with Band-Pass BW 18.0-40.0 GHz. in K to Ka band.

Insertion loss 2.0 dB

VSWR< 1.8

Pass-band Ripple is 0.5

Broad VSWR BW and Band-Pass BW of the filter can be designed using broadside offset coupled resonator elements in SSL medium as shown in Figure 4.2 (a). It is studied that VSWR BW and Band-Pass BW of the SSL structure using single section strip resonators in broadside offset coupled configuration is highest when the width of the same is narrowest as possible within the limit of practical fabrication and length the same is slightly less than quarter wavelength at the frequency of operation. It has also been studied that fabrication accuracies are ultimate limitation that needs to be considered for realization of the design and practical fabrication of the SSL BPF under consideration.

Here the number of parameters that need to be designed /optimized are high such as strip dimensions (width, length), offset gap between broadside strips, coupling gap between each edge coupled sections, relative permittivity (ε_r), thickness of substrate material, coupling coefficient, geometrical dimensions like normalized cavity height, width and the output parameters are effective permittivity (ε_{eff}), characteristic impedance (Z_0), width, length of strips. Here required number of resonators (broadside offset coupled section of strips) and physical dimensions for each of them, coupling gap between adjacent resonators have been computed theoretically [84-85] from required band-pass BW, coupling coefficients and accordingly the resonators are designed to achieve the same.

Initial design of the filter under consideration has been made using classical design process [78,83-84] using SSL structure that support fundamental propagating mode (TEM) as shown in Figure 4.2(b). Theoretical design has been done to compute physical dimensions of the SSL channel for dominant TEM mode propagation up to 60.28 GHz as listed below.

Channel Width (w) = 2.4 mm.

Channel Height (h) = 1.0 mm.

Dielectric Constant of the SSL Substrate (ε_r) = 2.2.

Substrate Thickness (t) = 5 mil.

Here a general synthesis method is followed for design of the filter [75-77,80,83-84] and it is observed that design and optimization techniques for enhancement of VSWR BW and Band-Pass BW of the BPF under consideration are required. Here the objective of the research work is to develop an optimal BPF having broad VSWR BW and Band-Pass BW where AI techniques are used in place of EM simulation tools. It is also required that accuracies of final design remains within the tolerance level of practical fabrication and measurement resources available to the author.

Depending on practical fabrication restrictions imposed on parameters of SSL channel, physical dimensions of single section strip resonators are computed and found not sufficient to cover K to Ka band (18.0-40.0 GHz.).It is observed that VSWR BW and Band-Pass BW of the SSL filter having single section broadside offset coupled resonator is restricted to more or less 10.0% surrounding its resonance frequency. It is also observed that if numbers of filter sections are increased the frequency response of SSL filter can be designed within the frequency range 18.0-40.0 GHz.

To design SSL BPF having VSWR BW and Band-Pass BW within the frequency range 18.0-40.0 GHz 15 section broadside offset coupled resonators are designed, integrated using edge coupled configuration and realized using SSL medium. In this design process Chebyshev response having 0.5 dB ripple in the pass-band is considered.

Here spectral domain techniques [73] are used for theoretical computations of physical dimensions of broadside offset coupled strip resonators [84-85]. A MATLAB code is developed to compute data for physical dimensions of the SSL resonators according to the coupling coefficients and SSL channel dimensions. ANN model of resonators for this SSL filter is designed and further used for development and optimization of the same within the frequency range. Spectral domain techniques are used to compute data for physical dimensions of SSL resonators for different frequency points within 18.0-40.0 GHz and used for training /testing of the ANN model under consideration over the frequency band.

The research work is carried out to develop trained and tested ANN model of the individual resonator sections of the SSL filter under consideration. Further optimization of VSWR BW and Pass BW of the SSL filter using trained/tested ANN model of the same and GA algorithm has been carried out. As a result of optimization modification of dimensions of the resonators are observed and is verified by the EM simulation tools. The dimensions of optimal SSL filter are computed from its trained ANN-GA model and technical details of design and optimization process are covered in different sections of this chapter of the thesis.

4.4 DESIGN OF ANN MODEL OF SSL RESONATORS

Second step for this design process is to develop an artificial model of the filter under consideration using NN to predict accurately the physical dimensions of strip elements within the tolerance level of fabrication accuracies. Design of the ANN model of resonator sections of the SSL filter is required for computation of input/output parameters of the same [124-127]. Here output parameters of this ANN model of offset coupled resonator sections are physical dimensions of the same and input parameters are coupling coefficient between individual resonator sections and dimensions of SSL channel.

Here four layers ANN having two hidden layers are chosen to model 15 different resonator sections of the SSL filter. Use of more number of neurons and number of hidden layers not only increases memory requirements but also there is a limit over which even if number of layers/neurons increases the accuracy of the ANN model will not increase at all. For the design of the ANN model of the SSL filter under consideration the number of neurons are chosen as 5 for the input layer, 10 and 6 for the first and the second hidden layers, 2 for the output layer. The tangent sigmoid activation functions is used in the first hidden layer. The log-sigmoid activation function is used in the input and output layers of the NN models for the SSL filter.

The training data for ANN model of the SSL filter is obtained from spectral domain analysis of offset coupled strips to compute its physical dimensions as performed by the author [74, 84-85]. In this design 940 data points randomly distributed in the frequency band of interest are used as training data for ANN model of resonator sections of the SSL filter. After proper training and testing ANN model of the same is used to find out the physical dimension of the resonator sections. Modeling accuracy of the filter parameters like physical dimensions of strips as obtained from trained and tested ANN model is tabulated in Table 4.1.

It is observed that accurate design of SSL resonators are required for the development of the BPF having filter response in the frequency range 18.0-40.0 GHz. Using trained ANN model of the resonators of the BPF under consideration required dimensional accuracies for strip width is 0.001 and the same for strip length is 0.0001 are computed. For accurate modeling and best possible prediction of design parameters of resonator sections of the ANN model, Lavenberg-Marquardt algorithm has been used here. The design data obtained from the trained and tested ANN model of the resonator sections of SSL filter is shown in Table 4.2.

Figure 4.3 shows the layout of 15 section gap coupled strip resonators of this SSL filter (2D and 3D views). The SSL filter under consideration (having fifteen resonator sections) is developed where the individual quarter wavelength resonator sections are coupled through a gap of 0.2 mm along the length (40.0 mm). The frequency depended S parameters of this SSL filter are computed using EM simulation. For enhancement of VSWR BW and Band-Pass BW of the SSL BPF, dimensions of 15 different resonator sections as computed from the trained ANN model of the same are modified using GA to optimize frequency depended reflectance and transmittance of the same over the frequency band.

4.5 OPTIMIZATION OF SSL FILTER USING GA

The third step of this design and optimization process [124-127] is to maximize the VSWR BW and Band-Pass BW of this SSL filter using ANN-GA algorithms and it is observed that trained and tested ANN model of each resonator of the SSL filter can be used with the GA optimization technique to optimize the same.

The physical dimensions of offset coupled resonators are output parameters of the trained ANN model under consideration and are changed according to the optimization algorithm using GA. The BW of reflectance and transmittance of this SSL filter are enhanced with modified dimensions of offset coupled resonators as obtained from trained ANN model and GA algorithm. The optimal design of the SSL filter as computed from its ANN-GA model is used to develop the same having optimum VSWR BW and Pass BW over the frequency range 18.0-40.0 GHz.

A cost function is selected and used to optimize the transmittance and reflectance BW of the SSL filter. In this process the cost function defined in Equation 4.1 is used for GA to compute physical dimension of each resonator of the SSL filter under consideration for optimum VSWR BW and Band-Pass BW of the same.

N represents the number of sampling points and w_i is the corresponding weighting value for the i-th sampling point. The cost function F is used here for GA optimizer for this optimization problem is maximize F where

$$F = \sum_{i=1}^{N} w_i f_i$$

(4.1)

f_i is related to S_{21} of the SSL filter under concern.

Optimized physical dimensions of 15 section broadside offset coupled strip resonators are computed for 18.0-40.0 GHz frequency band using ANN-GA model of the same and are is utilized for design the SSL BPF as shown in Figure 4.4. HFSS has been used to simulate the frequency response of S parameters of the 15 section SSL filter within the frequency range under consideration using the optimized (ANN-GA) physical dimensions of resonator sections. Figure 4.4 shows the 2D view of the layout of the SSL filter having 15 resonator sections with dimensions computed for the optimal design of the same.

4.6 SIMULATED RESULTS

The fourth step of this work is to compute the frequency response of transmittance and reflectance of the SSL filter using EM simulation (HFSS). Figure 4.5 shows the simulation results of frequency dependent S parameters of the SSL filter where trained and tested ANN model is utilized to generate physical dimensions of 15 different resonator sections.

Optimized (with GA) physical dimension of 15 resonator sections of SSL filter are used to design the optimal BPF for fabrication. Table 4.3 shows a comparison of the physical dimensions of resonator sections of this SSL filter before and after optimization. The physical dimensions computed from the ANN-GA model of the resonator sections of the SSL filter are used to compute frequency depended transmittance and reflectance of the optimal BPF using simulation as shown in Figure 4.6.

The simulated pass bands of optimal filter are observed to be within the frequency range 18.0 GHz - 41.0 GHz with an insertion loss of 0.5 dB (maximum) over the operating band. Start frequency of FEM simulation is 15.0 GHz. It is observed that deviation of simulated frequency response of the SSL filter as computed theoretically (Figure 4.5) and that obtained from its ANN-GA model (Figure 4.6) is due to approximation involved in ANN modeling.

It is observed that dimensional accuracies higher than 4.0mil are permissible for practical realization and this imposes limitations for practical fabrication of strip resonator using the SSL channel at 18.0-40.0 GHz. The dimensions of few resonator sections of optimized SSL filter are less than4.0 mil and have been approximated. Table 4.4 shows the physical dimensions of the each resonator section of this SSL filter used for fabrication. The effect of inserting 0.2 mm gap between two consecutive resonators is observed to alter the cutoff frequencies and to lower the operating frequency band slightly. To compensate the effect of the gap capacitance the resonator length can be scaled down appropriately. Alternatively the target design frequency may be kept at higher value to maintain the filter response for the desired operating band. EM simulation has been used to compute the frequency response of S parameters and other parameters of this SSL filter where the approximated optimized dimensions of 15 resonator sections of SSL filter are considered. Figure 4.7 shows the simulated (HFSS) frequency response of S_{21} and S_{11} of the SSL BPF under consideration using resonator dimensions (practically possible to achieve as shown in Table 4.4) of the individual resonator sections.

4.7 DEVELOPMENT OF SSL FILTER

Optimized physical dimensions of the resonators as obtained from the ANN-GA model of the SSL filter are approximated for practical fabrication and used to construct the same. It has been observed that the required accuracy in dimensions(width, length) of the strip elements to achieve broad BW of S_{21} and S_{11} parameters of this filter is 0.001 mm. Using best available fabrication facilities the tolerance of fabrication of such resonators are less than that required by the optimized design.

The final filter layout is shown in Figure 4.3 (b) and in Figure 4.4 where the approximated dimensions of resonators obtained from optimal design using ANN-GA model of the SSL filter has been considered and best achievable fabrication accuracy are used to generate the layout. Considering practical fabrication issues (i) CNC milling has been used to fabricate the SSL channel, (ii) bonding of the PCB containing resonator elements is done with the SSL channel and (iii) K connector is used to integrate the filter for characterization. All these pre measurement steps are required to be precise in order to get desired frequency BW of this optimized SSL filter.

4.8 MEASURED RESULT

The fabricated SSL filter as shown in Figure 4.3(c) is characterized using VNA (8575D) for measurement of the frequency response of the S parameters of the same. The measurement facilities at SAMEER, Kolkata, I.R.P.E. Calcutta University and AIACT&R, Delhi have been used for accurate measurement of the fabricated filter. Electronic calibration kit was used for calibration and it is observed that soldering and bonding losses of K connector, losses of semi rigid cables at 40.0 GHz. plays significant role in deciding S_{11} and S_{21} parameters of this filter. Fabrication and measurement accuracies are included in Table 4.5.The measured frequency response of S parameters of the fabricated SSL filter is compared with that of the theoretically computed ones and % deviation is computed.

Comparison of the simulated results with that of the measured results of the SSL filter is required to validate the design process. Measured BPF characteristics of the fabricated SSL filter and BW of reflectance and transmittance of the fabricated SSL BPF having 15 resonator sections are shown in Figure 4.8. The centre frequency of the developed SSL filter is 30.0 GHz and the measured range of frequencies for S_{11} and S_{21} of the BPF is observed to be within the frequency band from 18.0 GHz - 40.0 GHz. The frequency response of S parameters of the BPF as obtained from EM simulation and measurements are tabulated in Table 4.6 for comparison. Criterion used for computation of VSWR BW of the fabricated SSL filter are set as the range of frequencies having $|S_{11}| <$ -10.0 dB and that for Band-Pass BW of the fabricated SSL filter are set as the range of frequencies having $|S_{21}| >$ -5.0 dB.

The I.L. calculated from measured response of the SSL filter observed to be quite high compared to the simulated value. The discrepancies are coming due to fabrication inaccuracies of the strip elements and practical losses associated with connectors, cables and the filter fabrication process. Since there are additional losses due to shift of calibration and measurement plane, increased cable losses at 40.0 GHz and above, bonding and soldering loss due to K connector, insertion loss is 1.0 dB higher than S_{21} data over the full band. The loss can further be minimized using corrective measures.

The fabricated PCB has been tested under microscope having best available resolution and dimensions of resonator sections are found to be deviating by 30.0% from the precision of dimensions of optimized values(approximated) that required for fabrication of the same. Also the SSL channel dimensions are playing significant role in controlling the frequency response of the BPF. Measurement process of the filter has its own limitations due to measuring accessories, calibration of VNA and efficiency of operator involved in the same. The reference plane of measurement also plays an important role for deciding the frequency response. As a cumulative effect the measured frequency response of the filter are deviating much from those of simulation but can be improved using higher precision in fabrication processes.

77

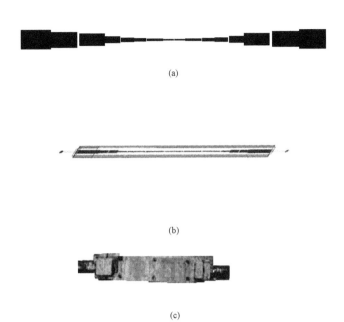

(a)

(b)

(c)

Figure 4.3 Fifteen section SSL filter (a) Artwork (b) 3D view of PCB (c) After fabrication

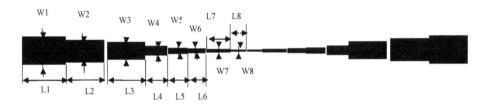

Figure 4.4 Optimized physical dimension of 15 section SSL filter (Obtained from ANN-GA model)

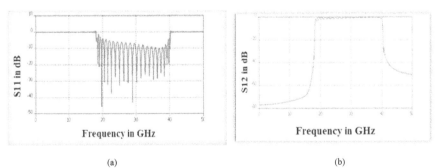

(a)   (b)

Figure 4.5 Frequency response performances of S parameters for SSL BPF (theoretically computed as in table 4.2) using simulation a) Frequency dependent reflectance, b) Frequency dependent transmittance

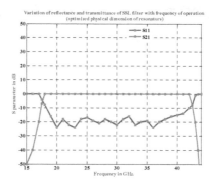

Figure 4.6 Simulated frequency response of S parameters of optimal SSL BPF as obtained from its ANN-GA model (dimensions as per Table 4.3)

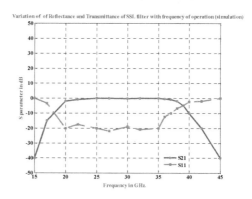

Figure 4.7 Simulated frequency responses of S parameters of SSL BPF where approximations are used for practical fabrication (using data from Table 4.4)

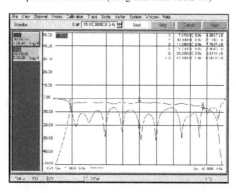

Figure 4.8 Measured frequency response of S parameters for fabricated SSL BPF

TABLE 4.1 Accuracy of ANN model of SSL resonator

Parameters of ANN model	Accuracies in terms of	Length of strip(mm)	Width of strip(mm)
Training	Average Error	0.0001	0.001
	Standard Deviation	0.02	0.9
Testing	Average Error	0.0001	0.001
	Standard Deviation	0.03	0.5

TABLE 4.2 Theoretically computed design of 15 sections SSL filter (symmetrical configuration)

Filter Sections	g values	Coupling Coefficients	Width of Strip(mm)	Length of Strip (mm)
1,15	1.7635	0.6361	0.2052	1.9039
2,14	1.2791	0.6238	0.1854	1.9052
3,13	2.6920	0.5426	0.0942	1.9125
4,12	1.3826	0.5278	0.0831	1.9135
5,11	2.7654	0.5227	0.0793	1.9138
6,10	1.3991	0.5204	0.0781	1.9139
7,9	2.7811	0.5193	0.0773	1.9140
8	1.4024	0.5189	0.0762	1.9141

TABLE 4.3 Dimension of broadside offset coupled strips before and after optimization

Filter Sections	Width of strip (mm) W		Length of strip (mm) L	
	Before optimization ANN model	After optimization ANN-GA model	Before optimization ANN model	After optimization ANN-GA model
W1, L1=1,15	0.2052	0.1999	1.9039	1.9035
W2, L2= 2,14	0.1854	0.1827	1.9052	1.9050
W3, L3=3,13	0.0942	0.0936	1.9125	1.9121
W4, L4=4,12	0.0831	0.0828	1.9135	1.9132
W5, L5=5,11	0.0793	0.0778	1.9138	1.9135
W6, L6=6,10	0.0781	0.0759	1.9139	1.9136
W7, L7=7,9	0.0773	0.0738	1.9140	1.9137
W8,L8=8	0.0762	0.0719	1.9141	1.9140

TABLE 4.4 Physical dimensions of strip resonators for fabrication of SSL filter

Filter Sections	1	2	3	4	5	6	7	8
Width of strip (mm)	W1 = 0.20	W2 = 0.18	W3 = 0.09	W4 = 0.08	W5 = 0.078	W6 = 0.075	W7 = 0.073	W8 = 0.071
Length of strip (mm)	L1=1.90	L2=1.91	L3=1.91	L4 =1.91	L5=1.91	L6=1.91	L7=1.91	L8=1.91

TABLE 4.5 Fabrication accuracies of SSL resonator

PRECESSION(MM.)	PHYSICAL DIMENSIONS OF FILTER PCB (MM)		% DEVIATION IN THEORETICAL AND PRACTICAL ACCURACIES	
	LENGTH	WIDTH	LENGTH	WIDTH
DESIGN	0.0001	0.001	0.01	0.28
FABRICATION	0.01	0.001	1.04	2.82
MEASURED (FABRICATED PCB)	0.02	0.01	2.09	28.2

TABLE 4.6 Comparison of simulated and measured performance of SSL filter

Filter Parameter	S PARAMETERS OF STRIP RESONATORS AT 30.0 GHZ			
	Simulated (Figure 4.6)		Measured (Figure 4.8)	
	S21	S11	S21	S11
	-22.0	-0.1	-18.5	-3.0
VSWR Bandwidth , S11 (-10.0 dB)	24.6 GHz (17.9-42.5)		22.0 GHz (18.0-41.0)	
Pass Bandwidth, S12 (-5.0 dB)	25.0 GHz(17.5-42.5)		24.5 GHz (17.5-42.0)	
Insertion loss	0.2 dB		3.5dB	

4.9 SUMMARY

ANN model of any repetitive unit of passive/devices can be designed, trained and tested using available data. The trained and tested ANN model of the BPF under consideration can be used further for computing the frequency response of the S parameters of the same up to certain accuracy. This is primarily useful for research lab and not for industries where critical specifications need to be fulfilled for delivery of the end product for practical systems. ANN models are useful to reduce i) time where repetitive design procedure is required; ii) cost involved in the design (workstation, software, manpower etc.). Complex designs can be implemented using several ANN models where the device response can be approximated within a short frequency range. Outside the range the ANN model is not valid and this design process is useful for those researchers who do neither have regular access to EM simulation software and nor have the expertise to analyze, design, develop devices/systems using commercial EM software or self written codes. So PG students and research scholars can use the proposed methodology for simulating those structures which do not have critical specifications. Some passive structures like Filter, Fractal Antenna, Directional Couplers, Microstrip Antenna etc. where design complexities are less, ANN model of the same can be i) trained to compute design parameters ii) combined with simulation tools to optimize design parameters of the structures under consideration within a certain frequency band.

It is easily possible to investigate different passive structures for optimal design using AI techniques and new findings up to the research level can further be validated by experimental processes. The author tries to establish the fact that students in research environment can utilize this technique to save time to repeat the design cycles as required for the case of EM simulation.

Here the applicability of ANN-GA technique to design passive filter and optimization of the same is demonstrated using one SSL filter. Here ANN technique is used to model resonator sections of the same and optimization process using GA is used to modify the dimensions of resonator sections for design of optimal BPF. The advantage of using trained ANN model of the same in place of EM simulator is reduction of time and design complexity. It is observed that resonator dimensions of SSL BPF can be computed from trained ANN model the same within 5-10 seconds using a standard PC (Pentium IV Processor, 2.0 GB RAM, 500.0 GB HD) whereas it requires 1-2 minutes to compute resonator dimensions of SSL BPF using EM simulator with PC having equivalent configuration. The computation speed is also dependent on configuration of the computing machine and once the ANN model is developed the data can be generated within few seconds as the computation becomes simple algebraic. For the case of EM simulation tools the design/optimization process is dependent on RAM and memory capacity of HD of the computing PC. Since complex solvers are used for simulation tools it requires few minutes to solve the EM field equations and generate the results.

It is observed that the accuracies of computations obtained trained ANN model are limited due to computation capability of the selected ANN model, training algorithm, testing accuracies etc. But design and optimization process using EM simulator (where appropriate resources are used to compute the optimal dimensions) is more accurate compared to trained ANN-GA algorithm but at the expense of higher cost. The AI technique can thus be used as an alternative procedure to design optimal filters particularly where costly EM software is not accessible.

5

OPTIMAL DESIGN OF A NOVEL MICROSTRIP FILTER

USING ANN-PSO TECHNIQUE

5.1 INTRODUCTION

Here research work is carried out to design and optimize a filter structure having multiple sections of ring resonators. A strong coupling structure is incorporated in the proposed design to obtain wide frequency band. The design parameters of the filter structure under consideration are modified for optimization of the VSWR BW and Band-Pass BW of the same. A Novel filter structure having multiple sections of ring resonators in microstrip configuration is considered and ANN-PSO model of the same is developed for optimization of the VSWR BW and Band-Pass BW of the same. In this process design parameters of the BPF structure under consideration are modified. Frequency response of reflectance and transmittance of the same are computed, simulated and compared with that obtained from fabricated BPF to validate the usefulness of the design/optimization procedure.

5.2 MICROSTRIP LINE CONFIGURATION

The microstrip transmission line structure as shown in Figure 5.1 is a conducting strip printed on a grounded dielectric substrate and surrounded by air. The EM field patterns of the structure are quasi TEM in nature as shown in Figure 5.2. The electric field lines have a discontinuity in the direction of wave propagation at the interface. The boundary conditions for electric fields are such that the normal component (the component at right angles to the surface) of the electric field times the dielectric constant is continuous across the boundary. The tangential component (parallel to the interface) of the electric field is continuous across the boundary. Since some of the electric energy is stored in the air and some in the dielectric, the effective dielectric constant of the microstrip transmission line structure is in between those of air and the dielectric. Typically the effective dielectric constant is 50.0-85.0% of the substrate dielectric constant. A high dielectric constant substrate reduces the radiation loss from the circuits. The power handling capability becomes restricted at the higher frequencies where the circuit dimensions are too small to be realized practically.

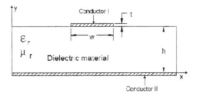

Figure 5.1 2D view of a microstrip line

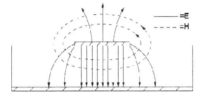

Figure 5.2 Electric (E) and Magnetic (M) field lines for fundamental Quasi-TEM in microstrip

5.3 MICROSTRIP BPF

It has been studied that design of a BPF with a pass band covering the UWB frequency range from 3.1 GHz -10.6 GHz (a FBW of 110.0%) according to FCC [86] with conventional filter designs techniques was a challenge to microwave filter designers and researchers. According to literature [87-113] FBW of more than 70.0% are reported for BPF before mid 2003 and found not covering the whole UWB frequency range. A BPF covering whole UWB frequency range with a FBW of 110.0% is one of the early reported filters [90-91] that possess an ultra-wide pass-band with high insertion loss. In 2004 a ring resonator with a stub was proposed which shows VSWR BW of 86.6% [92]. Here extensive research work has been carried out to design a microstrip filter having wide pass-band in the frequency range 3.1-10.6 GHz. and design/optimization procedure using AI technique are validated in the frequency band 3.1-10.6 GHz. The simulated design and measured result of the BPF under consideration is compared and found to be within the accuracy range of practical fabrication errors.

Researchers have proposed and developed many BPF having broad frequency band using different methodologies and structures [93-113]. A BPF with VSWR BW of more than 100% having very small dimensions was reported [103-112].Using different methods and structures filters having broad reflectance and transmittance has been developed as reported in the literature [116-123]. A planar BPF based on a microstrip structure can provide the advantages of easy integration with components, low cost, compact size and can be widely used in a variety of RF/microwave and millimeter wave systems. A tentative specification has been selected here for design, development and performance optimization of microstrip filter using AI technique. The research work has been initiated here to validate the design and optimization procedure of microstrip filter using ANN-PSO technique in place of EM simulator.

It is observed that for microstrip based filter configuration strong coupling between resonators are required in order to realize a broad pass band. Implementation of high coupling levels is also limited due to the resolution of the fabrication process. It was studied that using conventional microstrip parallel-coupled transmission line structure it is very difficult to achieve a wide pass-band for BPF. Size of the filter is also a factor and large size is undesirable in most of the applications.

5.4 ANN-PSO TECHNIQUES FOR DEVELOPMENT OF OPTIMAL MICROSTRIP RING FILTER

The objective of this work is to use the ANN model coupled with the PSO algorithm to optimize frequency response of S parameters of a five section microstrip filter using multiple ring resonators. Optimization of VSWR BW of the filter using AI technique without using EM simulation is the main focus of the research work covered in this chapter. A microstrip filter using ring configuration is designed, developed and optimized to justify the application of ANN-PSO techniques for development of optimal filter. Here design parameters of the filter structure under consideration are modified for optimization of the transmittance and reflectance of over a frequency band under consideration.

5.5 DESIGN AND OPTIMIZATION PROCESS OF MICROSTRIP RING FILTER

A systematic design and realization of a BPF in microstrip configuration is done using stub tuned ring shaped resonators having single input and single output [92,94-95]. In this work microstrip configuration (substrate thickness 10 mil, dielectric constant 9.8) is used to realize the filter using ring shaped resonator. The diameter of the ring is designed according to the resonating frequency and stub matching is used to tune the filter to the desired frequency band (UWB) of operation. The configuration of the filter structure having ring shaped resonator is shown in Figure 5.3 whose resonance frequency is tuned by a quarter wavelength short-circuited stub.

It has been observed that design and optimization procedure of the filter under consideration can be done with AI technique. EM simulation process for design and development of the filter can be replaced by a suitably designed, trained and tested ANN model of the ring resonator with connecting stub and the physical dimensions of the ring resonator and stubs can be modified according to optimization algorithm using PSO. Finally the reflectance and transmittance of the integrated microstrip ring filter can be obtained from the optimized ANN-PSO model of the ring resonator. The efforts has been done to validate the design and optimization procedure adapted here where frequency response of S parameters of optimal ring filter (integrated) has been computed using trained ANN model of individual ring resonator and optimization algorithm using PSO.

Here five coupled circular ring resonator with short circuited stubs are used to design the BPF structure. The characteristic impedances of ring resonators, short-circuited stubs and the characteristic impedances of the connecting lines are chosen for operation at 6.85 GHz (arithmetic mean of frequency range from 3.1-10.6 GHz). The ANN model of the ring resonators are designed for further optimization of VSWR BW and Band-Pass BW of the BPF under consideration and the schematic block diagram of the ANN model of the ring resonator is shown in Figure 5.4.

The physical dimensions of stub tuned ring resonators are used as input parameters of the ANN model of the same and frequency dependent transmittance and reflectance of each section of the ring resonator are output parameters. Here ANN model of the each section of the ring filter is trained and tested using data computed from theoretical analysis [110] using MATLAB. The PSO algorithm along with the trained ANN model of the ring resonator is used to optimize the frequency response of S parameters of the integrated BPF. Table 5.2 and 5.4 shows the set of design parameters chosen for the ANN model and that obtained from ANN-PSO model respectively.

In order to develop an optimal BPF using trained ANN model of the ring resonator the physical dimensions of stubs, ring diameter, connecting lines between each resonator are optimized. The optimized dimensions of the ring resonator and stubs are used to compute the frequency response of S parameters of the integrated BPF designed to work in the frequency range 3.1-10.6 GHz using EM simulator (IE3D)[138].

In order to optimize the filter parameters over the frequency range under consideration without using commercial EM simulation tools it is required to develop trained ANN model of the multi-ring BPF and suitable optimization algorithm like PSO. The alternative design and optimization process of the BPF under consideration using AI technique is a suitable replacement of EM simulation tools and can be established when the optimized design of the BPF using AI technique are realized and measured performance of the same are compared with that of the simulated one. Here efforts have been made to establish the utility of design/optimization process using ANN-PSO technique over the frequency range under consideration using microstrip ring filter.

5.6 RING FILTER CONFIGURATION

In this chapter details of design, optimization and characterization steps of a microstrip filter having multiple ring configurations are discussed. Detailed design and optimization process of an microstrip BPF are discussed in this section where the tentative specifications of the BPF is listed below

BPF with fractional bandwidth 3.1-10.6 GHz.(110.0 %).

Substrate 10 mil (Alumina)

Insertion loss <1.0 dB

VSWR< 2.0

The main goal of this research work is to design and optimize frequency dependent S parameters of a ring filter for use in the frequency band 3.1 GHz -10.6 GHz. Here ANN-PSO algorithm has been developed to compute optimum VSWR BW and Band-Pass BW of the proposed BPF. Typical filter parameters such as the R.L., I.L. and attenuation characteristics over the full frequency band are modified according to the optimization of the filter structure under consideration and steps to realize the optimal BPF are included in this chapter.

5.7 THEORY OF RING RESONATOR

Theoretical investigation and analysis of ring resonator using MOM is done to compute the non linear relationship of physical dimensions of ring structure with its S parameters. Theoretical investigation using MOM in the spectral domain [110] is carried out and further simulation using commercial software tools are performed to investigate the frequency response of S parameters for this multi-ring BPF. A MATLAB code is developed by the author using this theory as mentioned to relate the dimension of ring resonator with its frequency dependent reflectance and transmittance

5.8 DESIGN OF ANN MODEL OF RING RESONATOR

Here the aim of using soft computing technique is to compute the frequency dependent S-parameters of the ring filter using trained ANN model of the same without using EM simulation repetitively. The physical dimensions of the ring resonator along with the stub dimensions are taken as input design parameter for the ANN model of the ring filter and the frequency response in terms of S_{21} and S_{11} of the same are taken as the output parameters of the ANN model. In order to design, develop the trained ANN model of the ring BPF set of input and output parameters as listed in Table 5.1 are chosen for design of the same. It is observed that sufficient data is required to be generated for training the ANN model of ring filter. The theoretically computed data obtained from the spectral domain analysis [110] of the ring structure and implemented with MATLAB code is used to train and test the ANN model of the ring resonator within the frequency range 3.1-10.6 GHz.

A three layer ANN with a hidden layer having 16 neurons is used here to model each section of the ring filter. A training set of 670 randomly distributed value sets of the parameters in the range given in Table 5.2 is used to train the ANN model of each section of the ring filter. The back-propagation training algorithm along with the sigmoid function as the activation function is used for the feed-forward network of the ANN model in order to train it. The frequency dependent reflectance and transmittance of ring filter under consideration over the frequency range 3.1-10.6 GHz is obtained from its trained and tested ANN model. The accuracy of the trained ANN model is given in Table 5.4 in terms of average error and standard deviation.

The individual ring resonators with microstrip line stub having extended ground plane is designed and the overall frequency response of reflectance and transmittance is observed using simulation tool (IE3D) [138]. In this work micro strip substrate is used in order to realize the filter using ring resonator (substrate thickness 10 mil, dielectric constant 9.8).

The simulated frequency responses of transmittance and reflectance of a single ring resonator with tuning stub are found not to cover the frequency range of 3.1-10.6 GHz. To achieve more than 100% BW in the frequency range under consideration multiple section of ring resonators are required to be integrated to develop the BPF and frequency response of S parameters of the same are required to be optimized for obtaining VSWR BW and Band-Pass BW in the frequency band of operation.

Five ring resonators tuned with stubs are designed, developed and depending on the physical dimension of rings and stubs resonance frequencies of ring resonators are generated covering the frequency band under consideration. Five sections of ring resonator are combined to form the integrated ring filter. By controlling the input parameter of the trained ANN model of the ring resonator resonant frequencies of individual rings with shorting stubs can be designed/ tuned covering the frequency range 3.1-10.6 GHz. The trained ANN model of the each ring resonator is used to compute frequency dependent reflectance and transmittance data when design parameters of same are varied. Finally the integrated filter is developed combining five such resonator sections. The integrated ring filter configuration with the dimensions required for fabrication are shown in Figure 5.6-5.7 and can be used for enhancement of VSWR BW and Band-Pass BW as 150.0% or more. It is observed that by controlling the input parameters of the trained ANN model of the BPF under consideration the desired S-parameters can been obtained using optimization algorithm of PSO.

5.9 PSO OPTIMIZATION TECHNIQUE

The frequency depended reflectance and transmittance of the integrated ring filter is optimized using PSO for frequency band 3.1-10.6 GHz. The physical dimensions (width, length) of tuning stubs and resonators of the ring filter are obtained from its trained ANN model and are fed to PSO for optimization of transmittance and reflectance of the same. In order to optimize the ring BPF PSO algorithm is used with its trained ANN model and set of input and output parameters as listed in Table 5.1 are chosen for design of the same. A schematic block diagram illustrating the sequence of steps for design and optimization process using ANN-PSO algorithm is shown in Figure 5.5. A suitable cost function for PSO is used considering maximum transmittance and minimum reflectance of the micro strip ring filter and is shown below.

$$\text{Fitness} = \sum_{i=1}^{N} T_i - \sum_{i=1}^{N} R_i$$

$$T_i = \max\left(S_{21_i}, S_{21_D}\right)$$

$$S_i = \min\left(S_{11_i}, S_{11_D}\right)$$

$$T_i = \in S_{21_D} \qquad\qquad \forall S_{21_i} \leq S_{21_D} \;\&\; \forall S_{21_i} \geq S_{21_D}$$

$$\qquad\quad \in \min\left(S_{21_i}, S_{21_D}\right) \quad \text{otherwise}$$

$$R_i = \in S_{11_D} \qquad\qquad \forall S_{11_i} \leq S_{11_D}$$

$$\qquad\quad \in -S_i - \left|-S_{11_D} + S_i\right|^{Ki} \text{ otherwise}$$

where the subscript i indicates different simulated frequency points. N indicates the total number of simulated frequency points. S_{11_D} (in dB), S_{21_D} (in dB) are the design requirements for S_{11} and S_{21} respectively. The sign $\forall$ indicates that this operation is taken as soon as this condition is satisfied at all frequencies. K_i is set to 1 for all test cases in order to reach an equally weighted sum of reflection coefficient and transmission coefficient. The possible maximum sum of all R_i is - S_{11_D} *N. It can be achieved if all S_{11_i} are smaller than S_{11_D} .

The PSO algorithm converges within 50 iterations with sufficient accuracy. The optimized dimensions of the ring resonator and stubs used to tune the resonance frequency of individual rings are considered to fabricate the ring filter and optimized dimensions of geometrical parameters of the five section ring filter are tabulated in Table 5.5. The design parameters of ANN model of ring resonator and that of ANN-PSO model of ring filter are tabulated in Table 5.1 and illustrated using block diagram as shown in Figure 5.5.

5.10 DEVELOPMENT OF RING FILTER

The physical dimensions of resonator and stubs of integrated filter is optimized using ANN-PSO algorithm. EM simulation tool (IE3D) is used to compute the performance of this filter in terms of frequency response of reflectance and transmittance of the same. Simulated frequency response of transmittance and reflectance of the optimized five section ring filter is observed to be 3.3 GHz - 10.0 GHz as shown in Figure 5.8. It is observed that the accuracies of optimized design of the BPF are crucial to decide the filter response in terms of VSWR BW and Band-Pass BW.

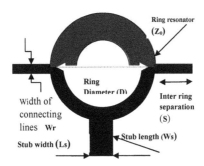

Figure 5.3 Artwork of filter configuration with single ring resonator having tuning stub

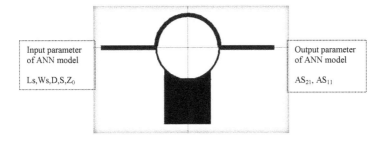

Figure 5.4 ANN model of single ring resonator with tuning stub

(Input and output design parameters of ANN model are indicated)

Figure 5.5 Schematic block diagram of ANN-PSO model of ring BPF

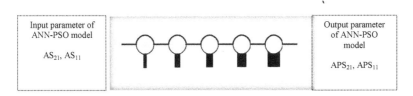

Figure 5.6 BPF configurations with five interconnected ring resonators with tuning stubs

(ANN-PSO model of ring filter with input and output design parameters)

The optimized design of the microstrip ring BPF is used for fabrication of the same. The simulated and measured frequency responses of ring filter are compared and tabulated in Table 5.5. The I.L. can be further reduced using low loss substrate and SMA connectors. The fabrication process is required to be precise to improve this loss figure and to cover the VSWR BW and Band-Pass BW from 3.1-10.6 GHz. Further the mounting of the filter is required to be rigid and full flatness of the substrate is required to be ensured to avoid surface wave loss.

5.11 CHARACTERIZATION OF RING FILTER

Based on the optimized design of the ring filter a layout is generated and fabricated using CER-10. In this process optimized physical dimensions of the geometrical parameters of the ring resonators (Table 5.4) are used with best possible fabrication precision available. The fabricated and integrated ring filter using optimized dimensions of geometrical parameters is shown in Figure 5.9.

The fabricated filter is measured for frequency response performance of S parameters (transmittance and reflectance) with the help of VNA (E8363B) and measured results show good filter characteristic over the frequency band 3.1-10.6 GHz. The measured attenuation and VSWR plot of the filter is shown in Figure 5.10 (a)-(b). The measured I.L. over the band is 3.0 dB (average) and measured BW of reflectance is 5.2 GHz. (4.3 GHz – 9.5 GHz) and BW of transmittance is 5.0 GHz. (4.5 GHz – 9.5 GHz) over the frequency band under consideration. A comparison of simulated and measured VSWR BW, Band-Pass BW and I.L. of the ring filter is shown in Table 5.5.

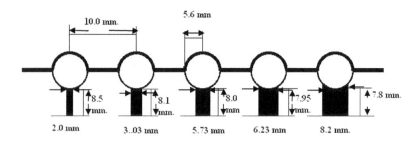

Figure 5.7 Artwork of microstrip BPF using multiple ring resonators with tuning stub

TABLE 5.1 Parameters of AI model of ring resonator

Design Parameters	ANN model of ring resonator	ANN-PSO model of ring filter
Input	Ls,Ws,D,S,Z_0	AS_{21}, AS_{11}
output	AS_{21}, AS_{11}	APS_{21}, APS_{11}

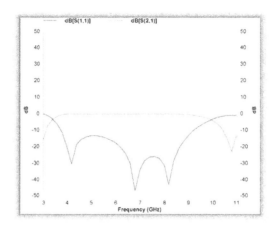

Figure 5.8 Frequency response of S parameter for ring BPF (EM simulation)

Figure 5.9 Fabricated microstrip ring BPF with five integrated ring

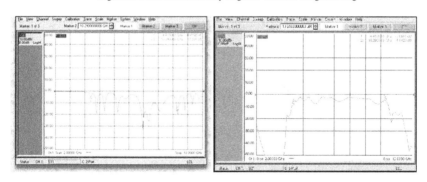

(a) Reflection measurement   (b) Transmission measurement

Figure 5.10 Measured frequency response characteristics of the ring filter (a) reflection measurement and (b) transmission measurement

It is observed that microstrip is a lossy structure and it is very difficult to be maintained the I.L. of the filter at 1.0 dB over the full frequency band The non-uniformity of the filter substrate (10 mil), its connetorization, radiation loss involved in sharp corners and lack of exact calibration of VNA are also responsible for loss figure of 3.0 dB in the measured result of this ring filter.

TABLE 5.2 Range of Input parameters for ANN model of the ring resonator

D(ring diameter) mm	Zo (Characteristic impedance of ring) ohm	S (Inter ring separation) mm	L(stub length) mm	W(stub width) mm
4.0-7.0	25-150	6.0-14.0	18.0-25.0	0.5-4.0

TABLE 5.3 Accuracy of developed ANN model of ring resonator

ANN Input/output Parameters	Ring dia.(mm)	Characteristic impedance of ring (mm)	Inter ring separation(mm)	Stub length(mm)	Stub width(mm)
Training	0.01	0.5	0.1	0.05	0.003
Average error	0.05	0.5	0.3	0.5	0.03
Testing	0.02	0.7	0.2	0.06	0.004
Average error	0.04	0.6	0.4	0.4	0.04

TABLE 5.4 Optimized dimensions of the ring resonator (ANN-PSO model)

D (ring diameter) 5.6 mm, Z_0 (Characteristic impedance of ring) 50 ohm, S (Inter ring separation) 10.0 mm

L (stub length) mm	S1 8.5	S2 8.1	S3 8.0	S4 7.9	S5 7.8
W (stub width) mm	W1 2.0	W2 3.0	W3 5.73	W4 6.23	W5 8.2

TABLE 5.5 Comparison of simulated and measured performance of the ring filter

Filter Parameter	Simulated(Figure 5.8)	Measured(Figure 5.10)
VSWR Bandwidth (-5.0 dB)	3.3-10.0 GHz	4.3-9.5 GHz
Band-Pass Bandwidth(-5.0 dB)	3.3-10.0 GHz.	4.5-9.5 GHz.
Insertion Loss	-1.0 dB	-3.0 dB

5.12 SUMMARY

The utility of using ANN model and PSO optimization technique for development of optimal filter is illustrated here with the help of microstrip ring BPF working in the UWB frequency range. A microstrip BPF with low insertion loss is designed and optimized for broad VSWR BW and Band-Pass BW using PSO.

Trained ANN model of the ring resonators with tuning stubs are designed and five different ring resonators are integrated to form the ring filter. The frequency response of reflectance and transmittance of the same are optimized using PSO where physical dimensions of individual rings/ tuning stubs, other parameters of the BPF configuration under consideration are modified to obtain the optimal design of the same.

Final filter layout is generated for fabrication with best possible fabrication precision available where optimized dimensions of the ring structure generated by ANN-PSO algorithm are used. The frequency dependent S parameters of the fabricated filter are measured to verify the frequency response performance of the same with the help of VNA and compared with that of the simulated performance. ANN-PSO technique is efficiently utilized here to achieve optimum VSWR BW and Band-Pass BW in terms of frequency dependent reflectance and transmittance of microstrip ring BPF working in the UWB frequency range.

The I.L. and measured VSWR BW and Band-Pass BW of the developed BPF are near to those of the desired value and can be improved further with some precautions. Other filter configuration can be considered for optimization where the ANN model, optimization parameters and the algorithm are different. It is observed that the once an ANN model is trained the optimization algorithm can be utilized efficiently for optimal design of filters in place of EM simulation tools within the frequency band under consideration. Using the developed ANN model frequency dependent S-parameters of ring filter for a given set of geometrical dimension of ring resonator/stubs in the frequency range of interest can be computed in negligible time.

In this process accuracy of the results, time required to achieve the optimal solutions, cost of resources required to obtain the same and expertise of the persons involved in the design process are key factors that need to be considered. Some compromise is required to obtain the same accuracy for the optimal design under consideration using optimization techniques like AI and its applications in place of EM simulation tools.

6

CONCLUSION

6.1 INTRODUCTION

In this chapter the main areas of research are emphasized and the new findings are highlighted as far as possible. Here specific aspects on which research work has been done using BPF configurations are briefly discussed. Ultimate goal of the research work is to establish the usefulness of soft computing algorithm for synthesis and optimization of BPF structures having different configurations which are analyzed, modeled and fabricated. As a validation of the proposed methodology three BPF structures are designed and developed to obtain broad VSWR BW and Band-Pass BW where AI techniques are utilized in place of EM simulation tools for optimal design of the same. In this thesis this concept has been illustrated where the measured results of fabricated BPF configurations under consideration are compared with that of the design/simulated results using AI techniques and discussed in earlier chapters (3-5). The research findings obtained so far on the basis of experimental results are discussed and future scope of work is included in this chapter too. The chapter ends with the directions for future research related to the topics discussed in the earlier chapter.

6.2 RESEARCH FINDINGS

Here soft computing techniques are utilized as a suitable alternative to existing filter design techniques and are discussed in details in chapter 2 of this thesis. Here computational techniques like trained ANN model along with GA/PSO algorithm are used for optimization of one waveguide, one SSL and one microstrip filters. The design, development and measurement results of fabricated filters are included in chapter 3-5 of this thesis. The applications of soft computing techniques in filter design and optimization process is demonstrated for different filter configurations where

(a) Waveguide BPF optimized for broad impedance BW at X band using ANN-GA technique. Here research involved in design of geometrical configuration of multi-post rectangular waveguide and the techniques used for optimal filter development are outcome of research and literature shows not much relevant research are published on this particular topic.

(b) SSL filter designed and optimized using GA algorithm for broad frequency band of operation (18.0 - 40.0 GHz) using trained ANN model of the same.

(c) Microstrip ring filter optimized for broad impedance BW from 3.1-10.6 GHz using ANN-PSO model. The optimal ring filter using microstrip configuration is developed where novel idea is used that has not been published earlier.

The optimization algorithms are used to fine tune the design and the hardware of the same are implemented using accessible resources, Fabricated BPF structures under consideration are measured to compare the performances with that of the optimized design. The new finding are published in reputed journals/conference proceedings and listed. The technical details of theory, design, development process, fabrication, measurements steps to validate the design process for each case are covered in chapter 3-5 of this thesis.

6.3 SUMMARY

There are standard techniques to model and synthesize microwave filters and various CAD methods can be used for development of optimal BPF. Here soft computing techniques (GA or PSO) are used as an alternative process for optimization of BPF. The trained ANN model of the same is used with GA/ PSO algorithm to optimize the frequency response of BPF.

A new configuration of waveguide filter is investigated where the design and optimization of the filter configuration is carried out using ANN-GA technique. The analysis of the structure and theoretical formulations using image theory, Lattice sum and T-matrix is carried out. A single cylindrical (conducting/dielectric) post centrally placed across the waveguide parallel to the electric field of the dominant mode is analyzed, modeled using ANN and multiple dielectric posts uniformly spaced inside X band rectangular waveguide in multi-layer configuration is observed to form BPF response. Here ANN and GA/ PSO techniques are used in place of EM simulators and this process can be utilized to design and optimize any filter.

Usefulness of ANN-GA technique for optimization of waveguide BPF using eight dielectric posts in four layer two-post configuration is established using measured result of the same. Detail discussions are covered in chapter 3 of this thesis. ANN-GA technique is also used to design an SSL filter where optimization, development and measurement of the same is carried out covering the frequency band 18.0-40.0 GHz. Broadside offset coupled resonators are used for synthesis of the filter and fifteen such resonator sections in edge coupled configuration are combined to design an optimal BPF under consideration.

The modal characteristic impedances and guide wavelength of offset coupled resonator sections are computed using spectral domain technique. Each resonator section of the SSL filter is modeled using ANN, trained using data computed using spectral domain techniques and is physical dimensions of the same are modified according to the optimization algorithm using GA. Here the trained ANN model is used to find out the physical dimension of the coupled strips as per the required coupling coefficients. Optimization for frequency response of S parameters of the filter is carried out using GA and optimized dimensions of fifteen broadside-offset coupled resonator sections are combined in edge coupled configuration to develop the BPF. Frequency response of the SSL filter in terms of VSWR BW and Band-Pass BW of BPF are computed using simulation tools. Here the BPF is realized at K to Ka band with Chebyshev response having 0.5 dB ripples in the pass-band. The SSL channel is designed for dominant TEM mode propagation. The optimized SSL filter is characterized for performance parameters, like the R.L., I.L. and attenuation characteristics. Here 79.3% VSWR BW of the filter with a reasonable I.L. is observed from the measurement results of the fabricated SSL filter.

A new innovative design of a micro strip based ring filter is designed, optimized and developed. Here basic resonator is microstrip ring configuration with stub used for frequency tuning and is optimized using ANN-PSO model for optimal transmittance BW and reflectance BW. Here ANN model is used for the synthesis of the ring filter using microstrip resonators. The PSO algorithm is used to optimize the filter geometry in order to obtain a wide VSWR BW and Band-Pass BW of the BPF using micro strip configuration.

The resonance frequency of a ring structure is controlled by a tuning stub whose design dimensions are computed using trained ANN model of resonator sections. The objective of this work is to use the ANN model coupled with the Particle Swarm Optimization (PSO) algorithm, to synthesize the microstrip filter using multiple rings and optimize its performance as broadband BPF. Theoretical analysis of the structure using MOM technique is done and further simulation using commercial software tools is performed to investigate the performance of the microstrip ring filter. The EM simulation results are in good agreement with those obtained using the ANN-PSO algorithm.

Five such ring resonator sections are integrated and a new configuration of microstrip ring filter is designed, optimized, fabricated and tested. The measured result as reported by the author shows 74.3% VSWR BW achieved in the FCC recommended UWB band with a -10.0 dB average R.L. over its pass band. These results indicate a very good agreement between simulation and measurements. However there is future scope to modify this design using asymmetrically coupled elements where fabrication difficulties can be further minimized.

6.4 FUTURE SCOPE OF WORK

Based on the research based work reported in the earlier chapters, several new ideas can be proposed.

(i)   The AI technique of optimization is very powerful for applications where iterative method is required to compute device parameters. Within a particular frequency range the ANN model can be properly trained with data available from theory and can be used for optimization using GA, PSO or other optimization techniques. A lot of research is going on with this focus and literature shows a number of publications on this subject. Passive as well as active devices can be modeled using this technique and using simple code the model can be utilized to get the best response possible from the structure. In this way a complex system can be separately model where initial response of each section can be combined to get overall response within a certain accuracy determined by the network topology and efficiency of the trained network to deliver output in the particular frequency of interest.

(ii)   The method adopted here for modeling and optimization is purely based on the mathematical computations which needs high end computing machines. The requirement is for computing resources (PC) having enough memory to store data and capability to link with other software to export and import the generated data in order to facilitate calculation process. Presently even the most basic personal computer can perform thousands of evaluations (or other calculations) per second for filters having 10 or more elements and can be directed through optimizer software. However the efficient training of the ANN depends on the number of neurons and the final accuracy of the output parameters of the model. So efficient computing platform is also a requirement in order to train the ANN model with a reasonable accuracy and further test it with the data available from theoretical analysis.

(iii)   Apart from filter, CPW circuits, Microstrip Antenna, FSS structure, etc can also be modeled efficiently using this approach. At high frequency the accuracy of the circuit response becomes high and this technique is not so effective in optimization problems beyond 20.0 GHz. However there are some modified algorithms available which can be used for circuit modeling in the frequency range of 20.0-30.0 GHz. This technique is not effective and seldom used for modeling or optimization problem above 40.0 GHz.

(iv)   The fabrication process of the waveguide filter involves complicated mechanical steps which lead to inaccuracies in some parameters of the filter assembly like position of the posts, their relative gap and alignment with respect to waveguide axis. Insertion of dielectric rod inside hollow waveguide creates some thin air gap at metal-dielectric junction and accurate modeling is required in order to model this imperfection which will be reflected in the final response as a loss term in R.L. and T.L. This can be minimized using conducting glue at the air dielectric interface and characterizing the effect of the glue on overall performance of the filter.

(v)   A new waveguide filter is proposed here for broadband BPF characteristics obtained from design modification and optimization. A new configuration of eight dielectric posts inside rectangular waveguide can have a BPF response and is discussed in chapter 3 of this thesis. The BPF and BSF nature of the waveguide filter with multiple dielectric posts can be further studied and new interesting findings may come out.

(vi)   The verification process can be extended for the other frequency bands (higher or lower) after proper optimization of the filter under consideration covering the respective frequency bands. But for upper frequency bands size of the waveguide become smaller, size of the dielectric rod decreases and the fabrication complication increases. The accuracy of the measured results deviates from the predicted performance. So it can be concluded that the application of this technique is well suited for passive devices below 18.0 GHz.

(vii)   The waveguide filter can be made tunable with external control on position of the dielectric posts and the tunability can be increased by using high dielectric constant material. BPF having elliptic frequency response can be achieved using this technology and can be optimized with a suitable software code or external tuning. This work can be extended to do some fundamental research on optimization related topics.

(viii)   The study of scattering and absorption of EM waves by multiple ferrite posts properly biased is also a topic of advanced research where filter response can be synthesized in a similar manner using ANN model and optimization is also possible using standard optimization techniques. This work can be further explored to design new configuration of BP and BS filters using ANN model and optimized to get optimal frequency responses.

    The MATLAB code that is developed for analysis of S parameters of multiple conducting or dielectric posts inside rectangular waveguide can be further extended to include higher order modal effects. The responses of active devices are much more nonlinear compared to passive devices like filters. In order to model the active devices over a particular frequency band required NN configuration becomes much more complex. Since the theoretical analysis of active devices are not so accurate in predicting their response, an alternative soft computing method using Neuro Genetic algorithm can be utilized for the design and optimization of passive and active devices. In this process the measured parameters of the device are feed as a training data of ANN model of the same. The trained and tested ANN model can be used with optimization tools for computation of device response over a frequency band within the accuracy of its developed ANN model.

APPENDIX

SCATTERING THEORY FOR CYLINDRICAL POST INSIDE RECTANGULAR WAVEGUIDE

A.1 Problem formulation

The geometry considered here is shown in Figure A.1 where two full height posts of circular cross sections with radii r_1 and r_2 are placed across the narrower dimension of the rectangular waveguide having dimensions a x b. The centers of two posts are located at $(\Delta_1, 0)$ and $(\Delta_2, 0)$ in the x-z coordinate, respectively. The posts may be dielectric or perfect conductor. The initial excitation is assumed to be $TE_{\mu 0}$ mode.

The Ey field of the incident wave propagating in the forward directions, viewed from the x_i-z (i=1,2) coordinate system, can be expressed using the cylindrical harmonic waves in rectangular coordinate systems as

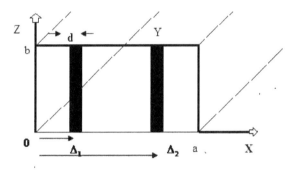

Figure A.1 Geometry of two full-height cylindrical posts placed across the narrower dimension of rectangular waveguide

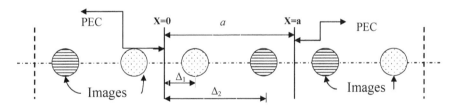

Figure A.2 Schematic view of cross sections of the original posts in a rectangular waveguide and the series of their images (configuration of two posts per unit cell).

$$E_{y,\mu}^i = a_\mu^+ \sin(k_{x,\mu} x) e^{ik_{z,\mu} z}$$

$$= -i\frac{a_\mu^+}{2}[e^{ik_{x,\mu}\Delta_i} e^{i(k_{x,\mu}x_i + k_{z,\mu}z)} - e^{-ik_{x,\mu}\Delta_i} e^{-i(k_{x,\mu}x_i - k_{z,\mu}z)}] \tag{A.1}$$

$$x_i = x - \Delta_i \quad (i = 1,2)$$

$$k_{z,\mu} = \frac{\mu\pi}{a}(\mu = 1,2,3...)$$

$$k_{z,\mu} = \sqrt{k^2 - k_{x,\mu}^2}, \quad \cos\theta_\mu = \frac{k_{x,\mu}}{k}$$

where $k_{z,\mu}$ is the propagation constant of the μ- th mode a_μ^+ is the amplitude of the incident field, k_0 is the wave number in free space. Using the cylindrical waves at the basis, Equation (A.1) can be written in the vectorial form.

$$E_{y,\mu}^i = \boldsymbol{\Phi}_i^T \cdot \mathbf{p}_{i,\mu}^+ a_\mu^+ \tag{A.2}$$

$$\boldsymbol{\Phi}_i = [J_m(k\rho_{i,0}) e^{im\phi_{i,0}}] \tag{A.3}$$

$$\mathbf{p}_{i,\mu}^+ = [p_{i,m\mu}^+] \tag{A.4}$$

$$p_{i,m\mu}^+ = \frac{1}{2}(-i)^{m-1}[e^{i(m\theta_\mu - k_{x,\mu}\Delta_i)} - (-1)^m e^{-i(m\theta_\mu - k_{x,\mu}\Delta_i)}] \tag{A.5}$$

$$k_{z,\mu} = \sqrt{k^2 - k_{x,\mu}^2}, \quad \cos\theta_\mu = \frac{k_{x,\mu}}{k} \tag{A.6}$$

$$\rho_{i,0} = \sqrt{(x - \Delta_i)^2 + z^2}, \quad \cos\phi_{i,0} = \frac{x - \Delta_i}{\rho_{i,0}} \tag{A.7}$$

where J_m is the mth order Bessel function, ($\rho_{i,0}, \phi_{i,0}$) denotes the polar coordinates with the origin at the centre of the ith post , the vector $\boldsymbol{\phi}_i$ and $p_{i,\mu}^+$ are defined as column vectors, the superscripts T denotes the transpose of the indicated vectors.

A.2 Expressions for scattered fields

Since the incident field and the post configuration are both uniform in the y direction the scattered field is also uniform in the y direction. Considering the series of infinite number of mirror images of the two posts with respect to two side walls as in Figure (A.2), the scattered field that satisfies the boundary conditions at x = 0 and x = a can be written as

$$E_y^s = \sum_{l=-\infty}^{\infty} \sum_{m=-\infty}^{\infty} X_{1,m} H_m^{(1)}(k\rho_{1,l}) e^{im\phi_{1,l}} - \sum_{l=-\infty}^{\infty} \sum_{m=-\infty}^{\infty} (-1)^m X_{1,m} H_m^{(1)}(k\rho'_{1,l}) e^{-im\phi'_{1,l}}$$

$$+ \sum_{l=-\infty}^{\infty} \sum_{m=-\infty}^{\infty} X_{2,m} H_m^{(1)}(k\rho_{2,l}) e^{im\phi_{2,l}} - \sum_{l=-\infty}^{\infty} \sum_{m=-\infty}^{\infty} (-1)^m X_{2,m} H_m^{(1)}(k\rho'_{2,l}) e^{-im\phi'_{2,l}} \qquad (A.8)$$

$$\rho_{i,l} = \sqrt{z^2 + (x - \Delta_i - lh)^2}, \quad \cos\phi_{i,l} = \frac{x - \Delta_i - lh}{\rho_{i,l}}, \quad h = 2a \quad (i = 1,2) \qquad (A.9)$$

$$\rho'_{i,l} = \sqrt{z^2 + (x + \Delta_i - lh)^2}, \quad \cos\phi'_{i,l} = \frac{x + \Delta_i - lh}{\rho'_{i,l}} \qquad (A.10)$$

where h=2a, $H_m^{(1)}$ is the m-th Hankel function of the first kind, $X_{i,m}$ is unknown amplitudes of the multi-pole fields scattered from i-th post, and ($\rho_{i,l}, \phi_{i,l}$) and ($\rho'_{i,0}, \phi'_{i,0}$) are the polar coordinates with their origin at (lh +Δi,0) and (lh -Δi,0), respectively.

The scattered fields expressed by Equation (A.8) are considered as fictitious periodic array of infinitely long and parallel circular cylinders within unit cell. The scattered field can be accurately calculated for a periodic array of cylindrical objects by the Lattice Sums technique. The analytical procedure is used to rewrite the Equation (A.8) is shown in section (A.3).

A.3 Calculation of four infinite sums of Bessel and Hankel function

First Term

$$\sum_{l=-\infty}^{\infty} \sum_{m=-\infty}^{\infty} X_{1,m} H_m^{(1)}(k\rho_{1,l}) e^{im\phi_{1,l}} = (\boldsymbol{\Phi}_1^{\mathrm{T}} \cdot \mathbf{L}^- + \boldsymbol{\Psi}_1^{\mathrm{T}}) \cdot \mathbf{X}_1 \tag{A.11}$$

$$\boldsymbol{\Psi}_1 = [H_m^{(1)}(k\rho_{1,0}) e^{im\phi_{1,0}}] \tag{A.12}$$

$$\mathbf{X}_1 = [X_{1,m}] \tag{A.13}$$

$$\mathbf{L}^- = [L_{mn}^-] \tag{A.14}$$

$$L_{mn}^- = S_{m-n}(kh), \quad h = 2a \tag{A.15}$$

$$S_{m-n}(kh) = \sum_{l=1}^{\infty} [1 + (-1)^{m-n}] H_{m-n}^{(1)}(lkh) \tag{A.16}$$

Second Term

$$-\sum_{l=-\infty}^{\infty} \sum_{m=-\infty}^{\infty} (-1)^m X_{1,m} H_m^{(1)}(k\rho'_{1,l}) e^{-im\phi'_{1,l}} = -(\tilde{\boldsymbol{\Phi}}_1^{\mathrm{T}} \cdot \mathbf{L}^+ + \tilde{\boldsymbol{\Psi}}_1^{\mathrm{T}}) \cdot \mathbf{X}_1 \tag{A.17}$$

$$\tilde{\boldsymbol{\Phi}}_1 = [J_m(k\rho'_{1,0}) e^{im\phi'_{1,0}}] \tag{A.18}$$

$$\tilde{\boldsymbol{\Psi}}_1 = [H_{-m}^{(1)}(k\rho'_{1,0}) e^{-im\phi'_{1,0}}] \tag{A.19}$$

$$\mathbf{L}^+ = [L_{mn}^+] \tag{A.20}$$

$$L_{mn}^+ = S_{m+n}(kh) \tag{A.21}$$

$$S_{m+n}(kh) = \sum_{l=1}^{\infty} [1 + (-1)^{m+n}] H_{m+n}^{(1)}(lkh) \tag{A.22}$$

Third Term

$$\sum_{l=-\infty}^{\infty} \sum_{m=-\infty}^{\infty} X_{2,m} H_m^{(1)}(k\rho_{2,l}) e^{im\phi_{2,l}} = (\boldsymbol{\Phi}_2^{\mathrm{T}} \cdot \mathbf{L}^- + \boldsymbol{\Psi}_2^{\mathrm{T}}) \cdot \mathbf{X}_2 \tag{A.23}$$

$$\boldsymbol{\Psi}_2 = [H_m^{(1)}(k\rho_{2,0}) e^{im\phi_{2,0}}] \tag{A.24}$$

$$\mathbf{X}_2 = [X_{2,m}] \tag{A.25}$$

Fourth Term

$$-\sum_{l=-\infty}^{\infty} \sum_{m=-\infty}^{\infty} (-1)^m X_{2,m} H_m^{(1)}(k\rho'_{2,l}) e^{-im\phi'_{2,l}} = -(\tilde{\boldsymbol{\Phi}}_2^{\mathrm{T}} \cdot \mathbf{L}^+ + \tilde{\boldsymbol{\Psi}}_2^{\mathrm{T}}) \cdot \mathbf{X}_2 \tag{A.26}$$

$$\tilde{\boldsymbol{\Phi}}_2 = [J_m(k\rho'_{2,0}) e^{im\phi'_{2,0}}] \tag{A.27}$$

$$\tilde{\boldsymbol{\Psi}}_2 = [H_{-m}^{(1)}(k\rho'_{2,0}) e^{-im\phi'_{2,0}}] \tag{A.28}$$

A.4 Expressions for the total field for forward propagating wave

The unknown amplitudes $\{X_{im}\}$ (i= 1,2) are determined so that the scattered fields satisfy the boundary conditions on the surfaces of two circular posts. This calculation is performed by using Equations (A.11), (A.17), (A.23) and (A.26). As the first step, all of the basis functions included in Equations (A.17), (A.23) and (A.26) are transformed into the ($\rho_{i,0}, \phi_{i,0}$) coordinate system using the Graf's addition theorem.

$$\tilde{\Phi}_1 = \tilde{\alpha}_1 \cdot \Phi_1 \tag{A.29}$$

$$\tilde{\Psi}_1 = \tilde{\beta}_1 \cdot \Phi_1 \tag{A.30}$$

$$\tilde{\Phi}_2 = \xi \cdot \Phi_1 \tag{A.31}$$

$$\tilde{\Psi}_2 = \eta \cdot \Phi_1 \tag{A.32}$$

$$\Phi_2 = \alpha_1 \cdot \Phi_1 \tag{A.33}$$

$$\Psi_2 = \beta_1 \cdot \Phi_1 \qquad \text{with} \tag{A.34}$$

$$\tilde{\alpha}_1 = [\tilde{\alpha}_{1,mn}] = [J_{m-n}(2k\Delta_1)]$$
$$\tilde{\beta}_1 = [\tilde{\beta}_{1,mn}] = [(-1)^{m+n} H_{m+n}^{(1)}(2k\Delta_1)] \tag{A.35}$$

$$\tag{A.36}$$

$$\xi = [\xi_{mn}] = [J_{m-n}(k\Delta^+)], \quad \Delta^+ = \Delta_1 + \Delta_2 \tag{A.37}$$

$$\eta = [\eta_{mn}] = [(-1)^{m+n} H_{m+n}^{(1)}(k\Delta^+)] \tag{A.38}$$

$$\alpha_1 = [\alpha_{1,mn}] = [(-1)^{m-n} J_{m-n}(k\Delta^-)], \quad \Delta^- = \Delta_2 - \Delta_1 \tag{A.39}$$

$$\beta_1 = [\beta_{1,mn}] = [(-1)^{m-n} H_{m-n}^{(1)}(k\Delta^-)] \tag{A.40}$$

where $\Delta^{\pm} = \Delta_1 + \Delta_2$ and $\tilde{\alpha}_1$ to β_1 denote the translation matrices for the cylindrical wave functions between the indicated two coordinated systems. Using Equations (A.29) – (A.34) in Equations (A.11), (A.17), (A.23) and (A.26) the total field may be expressed in terms of ($\rho_{1,0}, \phi_{1,0}$) coordinate system as discussed in the next section. Total field expressed on the basis of the ($\rho_{1,0}, \varphi_{1,0}$) coordinate

$$E_y = E_y^i + E_y^s$$

$$= \boldsymbol{\Phi}_1^{\mathrm{T}} \cdot \mathbf{p}_{1,\mu}^+ a_\mu^+ + (\boldsymbol{\Phi}_1^{\mathrm{T}} \cdot \mathbf{L}^- + \boldsymbol{\Psi}_1^{\mathrm{T}}) \cdot \mathbf{X}_1 - (\tilde{\boldsymbol{\Phi}}_1^{\mathrm{T}} \cdot \mathbf{L}^+ + \tilde{\boldsymbol{\Psi}}_1^{\mathrm{T}}) \cdot \mathbf{X}_1$$

$$+ (\boldsymbol{\Phi}_2^{\mathrm{T}} \cdot \mathbf{L}^- + \boldsymbol{\Psi}_2^{\mathrm{T}}) \cdot \mathbf{X}_2 - (\tilde{\boldsymbol{\Phi}}_2^{\mathrm{T}} \cdot \mathbf{L}^+ + \tilde{\boldsymbol{\Psi}}_2^{\mathrm{T}}) \cdot \mathbf{X}_2$$

$$= \boldsymbol{\Phi}_1^{\mathrm{T}} \cdot \mathbf{p}_{1,\mu}^+ a_\mu^+ + (\boldsymbol{\Phi}_1^{\mathrm{T}} \cdot \mathbf{L}^- + \boldsymbol{\Psi}_1^{\mathrm{T}}) \cdot \mathbf{X}_1 - \boldsymbol{\Phi}_1^{\mathrm{T}} \cdot (\tilde{\boldsymbol{\alpha}}_1^{\mathrm{T}} \mathbf{L}^+ + \tilde{\boldsymbol{\beta}}_1^{\mathrm{T}}) \cdot \mathbf{X}_1$$

$$+ \boldsymbol{\Phi}_1^{\mathrm{T}} \cdot (\boldsymbol{\alpha}_1^{\mathrm{T}} \mathbf{L}^- + \boldsymbol{\beta}_1^{\mathrm{T}}) \cdot \mathbf{X}_2 - \boldsymbol{\Phi}_1^{\mathrm{T}} \cdot (\boldsymbol{\xi}^{\mathrm{T}} \mathbf{L}^+ + \boldsymbol{\eta}^{\mathrm{T}}) \cdot \mathbf{X}_2$$

$$= \boldsymbol{\Phi}_1^{\mathrm{T}} \cdot [\mathbf{p}_{1,\mu}^+ a_\mu^+ + (\mathbf{L}^- - \tilde{\boldsymbol{\alpha}}_1^{\mathrm{T}} \mathbf{L}^+ - \tilde{\boldsymbol{\beta}}_1^{\mathrm{T}}) \cdot \mathbf{X}_1 + (\boldsymbol{\alpha}_1^{\mathrm{T}} \mathbf{L}^- + \boldsymbol{\beta}_1^{\mathrm{T}} - \boldsymbol{\xi}^{\mathrm{T}} \mathbf{L}^+ - \boldsymbol{\eta}^{\mathrm{T}}) \cdot \mathbf{X}_2] + \boldsymbol{\Psi}_1^{\mathrm{T}} \cdot \mathbf{X}_1$$

$$E_y = \boldsymbol{\Phi}_1^{\mathrm{T}} \cdot [\mathbf{p}_{1,\mu}^+ a_\mu^+ + (\mathbf{L}^- - \tilde{\boldsymbol{\alpha}}_1^{\mathrm{T}} \mathbf{L}^+ - \tilde{\boldsymbol{\beta}}_1^{\mathrm{T}}) \cdot \mathbf{X}_1 + (\boldsymbol{\alpha}_1^{\mathrm{T}} \mathbf{L}^- + \boldsymbol{\beta}_1^{\mathrm{T}} - \boldsymbol{\xi}^{\mathrm{T}} \mathbf{L}^+ - \boldsymbol{\eta}^{\mathrm{T}}) \cdot \mathbf{X}_2] + \boldsymbol{\Psi}_1^{\mathrm{T}} \cdot \mathbf{X}_1 \quad \text{(A.41)}$$

The first term in Equation (A.41) can be viewed as the incident field impinging on the circular post #1 located at $(\Delta_1, 0)$ in free space, whereas the second term impinging on the circular post #1 when isolated in free space. Then the following relation is used.

$$\mathbf{X}_1 = \mathbf{T}_1 \cdot [\mathbf{p}_{1,\mu}^+ a_\mu^+ + (\mathbf{L}^- - \tilde{\boldsymbol{\alpha}}_1^{\mathrm{T}} \mathbf{L}^+ - \tilde{\boldsymbol{\beta}}_1^{\mathrm{T}}) \cdot \mathbf{X}_1 + (\boldsymbol{\alpha}_1^{\mathrm{T}} \mathbf{L}^- + \boldsymbol{\beta}_1^{\mathrm{T}} - \boldsymbol{\xi}^{\mathrm{T}} \mathbf{L}^+ - \boldsymbol{\eta}^{\mathrm{T}}) \cdot \mathbf{X}_2] \quad \text{(A.42)}$$

Equation (A.42) yields the boundary condition for the scattered field on the surface of the post #1 expressed in terms of T-matrix.

A.5 Expressions for the total field for backward propagating wave

Next step of this analysis is performed by using Equations (A.11), (A.17), (A.23) and (AI.26). As the second step of analysis, all basis functions included in Equations (A.11), (A.17) and (A.26) are transformed into the $(\rho_{2,0}, \phi_{2,0})$ coordinate system using the Graf's addition theorem as

$$\tilde{\boldsymbol{\Phi}}_2 = \tilde{\boldsymbol{\alpha}}_2 \cdot \boldsymbol{\Phi}_2 \quad \text{(A.43)}$$

$$\tilde{\boldsymbol{\Psi}}_2 = \tilde{\boldsymbol{\beta}}_2 \cdot \boldsymbol{\Phi}_2 \quad \text{(A.44)}$$

$$\tilde{\boldsymbol{\Phi}}_1 = \boldsymbol{\xi} \cdot \boldsymbol{\Phi}_2 \quad \text{(A.45)}$$

$$\tilde{\boldsymbol{\Psi}}_1 = \boldsymbol{\eta} \cdot \boldsymbol{\Phi}_2 \quad \text{(AI.46)}$$

$$\boldsymbol{\Phi}_1 = \boldsymbol{\alpha}_2 \cdot \boldsymbol{\Phi}_2 \quad \text{(A.47)}$$

$$\boldsymbol{\Psi}_1 = \boldsymbol{\beta}_2 \cdot \boldsymbol{\Phi}_2 \qquad \text{where} \quad \text{(A.48)}$$

$$\tilde{\boldsymbol{\alpha}}_2 = [\tilde{\alpha}_{2,mn}] = [J_{m-n}(2k\Delta_2)] \quad \text{(A.49)}$$

$$\tilde{\boldsymbol{\beta}}_2 = [\tilde{\beta}_{2,mn}] = [(-1)^{m+n} H_{m+n}^{(1)}(2k\Delta_2)] \quad \text{(A.50)}$$

$$\boldsymbol{\alpha}_2 = [\alpha_{2,mn}] = [J_{m-n}(k\Delta^-)], \quad \Delta^- = \Delta_2 - \Delta_1 \quad \text{(A.51)}$$

$$\boldsymbol{\beta}_2 = [\beta_{2,mn}] = [H_{m-n}^{(1)}(k\Delta^-)] \tag{A.52}$$

Using Equations (A.43)-(A.48) in Equations (A.22), (A.28), (A.34) and (A.37) the total field may be expressed in terms of ($\rho_{2,0}, \phi_{2,0}$) coordinate system.

$$\begin{aligned}
E_y &= E_y^i + E_y^s \\
&= \boldsymbol{\Phi}_2^T \cdot \mathbf{p}_{2,\mu}^+ a_\mu^+ + (\boldsymbol{\Phi}_1^T \cdot \mathbf{L}^- + \boldsymbol{\Psi}_1^T) \cdot \mathbf{X}_1 - (\tilde{\boldsymbol{\Phi}}_1^T \cdot \mathbf{L}^+ + \tilde{\boldsymbol{\Psi}}_1^T) \cdot \mathbf{X}_1 \\
&\quad + (\boldsymbol{\Phi}_2^T \cdot \mathbf{L}^- + \boldsymbol{\Psi}_2^T) \cdot \mathbf{X}_2 - (\tilde{\boldsymbol{\Phi}}_2^T \cdot \mathbf{L}^+ + \tilde{\boldsymbol{\Psi}}_2^T) \cdot \mathbf{X}_2 \\
&= \boldsymbol{\Phi}_2^T \cdot \mathbf{p}_{2,\mu}^+ a_\mu^+ + \boldsymbol{\Phi}_2^T \cdot [(\boldsymbol{\alpha}_2^T \mathbf{L}^- + \boldsymbol{\beta}_2^T) \cdot \mathbf{X}_1 - (\boldsymbol{\xi}^T \mathbf{L}^+ + \boldsymbol{\eta}^T) \cdot \mathbf{X}_1 \\
&\quad + (\mathbf{L}^- - \tilde{\boldsymbol{\alpha}}_2^T \mathbf{L}^+ - \tilde{\boldsymbol{\beta}}_2^T) \cdot \mathbf{X}_2 + \boldsymbol{\Psi}_2^T \cdot \mathbf{X}_2 \\
&= \boldsymbol{\Phi}_2^T \cdot [\mathbf{p}_{2,\mu}^+ a_\mu^+ + (\mathbf{L}^- - \tilde{\boldsymbol{\alpha}}_2^T \mathbf{L}^+ - \tilde{\boldsymbol{\beta}}_2^T) \cdot \mathbf{X}_2 + (\boldsymbol{\alpha}_2^T \mathbf{L}^- + \boldsymbol{\beta}_2^T - \boldsymbol{\xi}^T \mathbf{L}^+ - \boldsymbol{\eta}^T) \cdot \mathbf{X}_1] + \boldsymbol{\Psi}_2^T \cdot \mathbf{X}_2
\end{aligned}$$

$$E_y = \boldsymbol{\Phi}_2^T \cdot [\mathbf{p}_{2,\mu}^+ a_\mu^+ + (\mathbf{L}^- - \tilde{\boldsymbol{\alpha}}_2^T \mathbf{L}^+ - \tilde{\boldsymbol{\beta}}_2^T) \cdot \mathbf{X}_2 + (\boldsymbol{\alpha}_2^T \mathbf{L}^- + \boldsymbol{\beta}_2^T - \boldsymbol{\xi}^T \mathbf{L}^+ - \boldsymbol{\eta}^T) \cdot \mathbf{X}_1] + \boldsymbol{\Psi}_2^T \cdot \mathbf{X}_2 \tag{A.53}$$

The first term in Equation (A.53) can be viewed as the incident field impinging on the circular post #1 located at $(\Delta, 0)$ in free space, whereas the second term is the incident field impinging on the circular post #1 when isolated in free space. Then the following relation is used.

$$\mathbf{X}_2 = \mathbf{T}_2 \cdot [\mathbf{p}_{2,\mu}^+ a_\mu^+ + (\mathbf{L}^- - \tilde{\boldsymbol{\alpha}}_2^T \mathbf{L}^+ - \tilde{\boldsymbol{\beta}}_2^T) \cdot \mathbf{X}_2 + (\boldsymbol{\alpha}_2^T \mathbf{L}^- + \boldsymbol{\beta}_2^T - \boldsymbol{\xi}^T \mathbf{L}^+ - \boldsymbol{\eta}^T) \cdot \mathbf{X}_1] \tag{A.54}$$

Equation (A.54) yields the boundary condition for the scattered fields expressed in terms of T-matrix. When equation (A.42) and (A.54) are simultaneously satisfied, the scattered field expressed by Equation (A.1) satisfies the boundary conditions on the surface of the posts #1 and #2 . Solving Equations (A.42) and (A.54) after straight forward manipulations, the unknown amplitude vectors X_1 and X_2 are determined as follows.

$$\mathbf{X}_1 = \bar{\bar{\mathbf{T}}}_1 \bar{\bar{\mathbf{K}}}_1 \cdot \mathbf{X}_2 + \bar{\bar{\mathbf{T}}}_1 \cdot \mathbf{p}_{1,\mu}^+ a_\mu^+ \tag{A.55}$$

$$\mathbf{X}_2 = \bar{\bar{\mathbf{T}}}_2 \bar{\bar{\mathbf{K}}}_2 \cdot \mathbf{X}_1 + \bar{\bar{\mathbf{T}}}_2 \cdot \mathbf{p}_{2,\mu}^+ a_\mu^+ \quad \text{where} \tag{A.56}$$

$$\bar{\bar{\mathbf{T}}}_i = (\mathbf{I} - \mathbf{T}_i \cdot \mathbf{L}_i)^{-1} \cdot \mathbf{T}_i \quad (i = 1, 2) \tag{A.57}$$

$$\mathbf{L}_i = \mathbf{L}^- - \tilde{\boldsymbol{\alpha}}_i^T \cdot \mathbf{L}^+ - \tilde{\boldsymbol{\beta}}_i^T \tag{A.58}$$

$$\bar{\bar{\mathbf{K}}}_1 = \boldsymbol{\alpha}_1^T \mathbf{L}^- + \boldsymbol{\beta}_1^T - \boldsymbol{\xi}^T \mathbf{L}^+ - \boldsymbol{\eta}^T \tag{A.59}$$

$$\bar{\bar{\mathbf{K}}}_2 = \boldsymbol{\alpha}_2^T \mathbf{L}^- + \boldsymbol{\beta}_2^T - \boldsymbol{\xi}^T \mathbf{L}^+ - \boldsymbol{\eta}^T \tag{A.60}$$

$\mathbf{T}_i$: T-matrix of the isolated i-th circular cylinder in free space

$\overline{\overline{\mathbf{T}}}_i$: T-matrix of the i-th circular post in rectangular waveguide including the mutual interaction between the two posts.

$$
\left(
\begin{aligned}
&\mathbf{X}_1 = \overline{\overline{\mathbf{T}}}_1\overline{\overline{\mathbf{K}}}_1 \cdot \mathbf{X}_2 + \overline{\overline{\mathbf{T}}}_1 \cdot \mathbf{p}^+_{1,\mu}a^+_\mu = \overline{\overline{\mathbf{T}}}_1\overline{\overline{\mathbf{K}}}_1 \cdot [\overline{\overline{\mathbf{T}}}_2\overline{\overline{\mathbf{K}}}_2 \cdot \mathbf{X}_1 + \overline{\overline{\mathbf{T}}}_2 \cdot \mathbf{p}^+_{2,\mu}a^+_\mu] + \overline{\overline{\mathbf{T}}}_1 \cdot \mathbf{p}^+_{1,\mu}a^+_\mu \\
&(\mathbf{I} - \overline{\overline{\mathbf{T}}}_1\overline{\overline{\mathbf{K}}}_1\overline{\overline{\mathbf{T}}}_2\overline{\overline{\mathbf{K}}}_2) \cdot \mathbf{X}_1 = \overline{\overline{\mathbf{T}}}_1\overline{\overline{\mathbf{K}}}_1\overline{\overline{\mathbf{T}}}_2 \cdot \mathbf{p}^+_{2,\mu}a^+_\mu + \overline{\overline{\mathbf{T}}}_1 \cdot \mathbf{p}^+_{1,\mu}a^+_\mu \\
&\mathbf{X}_1 = (\mathbf{I} - \overline{\overline{\mathbf{T}}}_1\overline{\overline{\mathbf{K}}}_1\overline{\overline{\mathbf{T}}}_2\overline{\overline{\mathbf{K}}}_2)^{-1}\overline{\overline{\mathbf{T}}}_1 \cdot (\overline{\overline{\mathbf{K}}}_1\overline{\overline{\mathbf{T}}}_2 \cdot \mathbf{p}^+_{2,\mu} + \mathbf{p}^+_{1,\mu})a^+_\mu \\
&\mathbf{X}_2 = (\mathbf{I} - \overline{\overline{\mathbf{T}}}_2\overline{\overline{\mathbf{K}}}_2\overline{\overline{\mathbf{T}}}_1\overline{\overline{\mathbf{K}}}_1)^{-1}\overline{\overline{\mathbf{T}}}_2 \cdot (\overline{\overline{\mathbf{K}}}_2\overline{\overline{\mathbf{T}}}_1 \cdot \mathbf{p}^+_{1,\mu} + \mathbf{p}^+_{2,\mu})a^+_\mu
\end{aligned}
\right)
\tag{A.61}
$$

where it is assumed that

$$
\mathbf{X}_1 = (\mathbf{I} - \overline{\overline{\mathbf{T}}}_1\overline{\overline{\mathbf{K}}}_1\overline{\overline{\mathbf{T}}}_2\overline{\overline{\mathbf{K}}}_2)^{-1}\overline{\overline{\mathbf{T}}}_1 \cdot (\overline{\overline{\mathbf{K}}}_1\overline{\overline{\mathbf{T}}}_2 \cdot \mathbf{p}^+_{2,\mu} + \mathbf{p}^+_{1,\mu})a^+_\mu = (\mathbf{S}_{11} \cdot \mathbf{p}^+_{1,\mu} + \mathbf{S}_{12} \cdot \mathbf{p}^+_{2,\mu})a^+_\mu
\tag{A.62}
$$

$$
\mathbf{X}_2 = (\mathbf{I} - \overline{\overline{\mathbf{T}}}_2\overline{\overline{\mathbf{K}}}_2\overline{\overline{\mathbf{T}}}_1\overline{\overline{\mathbf{K}}}_1)^{-1}\overline{\overline{\mathbf{T}}}_2 \cdot (\overline{\overline{\mathbf{K}}}_2\overline{\overline{\mathbf{T}}}_1 \cdot \mathbf{p}^+_{1,\mu} + \mathbf{p}^+_{2,\mu}]a^+_\mu = (\mathbf{S}_{21} \cdot \mathbf{p}^+_{1,\mu} + \mathbf{S}_{22} \cdot \mathbf{p}^+_{2,\mu})a^+_\mu \quad \text{with}
\tag{A.63}
$$

$$
\begin{aligned}
\mathbf{S}_{11} &= (\mathbf{I} - \overline{\overline{\mathbf{T}}}_1\overline{\overline{\mathbf{K}}}_1\overline{\overline{\mathbf{T}}}_2\overline{\overline{\mathbf{K}}}_2)^{-1}\overline{\overline{\mathbf{T}}}_1 \\
\mathbf{S}_{12} &= (\mathbf{I} - \overline{\overline{\mathbf{T}}}_1\overline{\overline{\mathbf{K}}}_1\overline{\overline{\mathbf{T}}}_2\overline{\overline{\mathbf{K}}}_2)^{-1}\overline{\overline{\mathbf{T}}}_1\overline{\overline{\mathbf{K}}}_1\overline{\overline{\mathbf{T}}}_2
\end{aligned}
\tag{A.64}
$$

$$
\begin{aligned}
\mathbf{S}_{21} &= (\mathbf{I} - \overline{\overline{\mathbf{T}}}_2\overline{\overline{\mathbf{K}}}_2\overline{\overline{\mathbf{T}}}_1\overline{\overline{\mathbf{K}}}_1)^{-1}\overline{\overline{\mathbf{T}}}_2\overline{\overline{\mathbf{K}}}_2\overline{\overline{\mathbf{T}}}_1 \\
\mathbf{S}_{22} &= (\mathbf{I} - \overline{\overline{\mathbf{T}}}_2\overline{\overline{\mathbf{K}}}_2\overline{\overline{\mathbf{T}}}_1\overline{\overline{\mathbf{K}}}_1)^{-1}\overline{\overline{\mathbf{T}}}_2
\end{aligned}
\tag{A.65}
$$

where $\overline{\overline{\mathbf{T}}}_i$: (i=1,2) represents the aggregate T-matrix of post #i located in the rectangular waveguide, which satisfies the boundary conditions at x = 0 and x = a, L_i is the aggregate lattice-sums matrix for a periodic arrangement of infinite number of mirror images of post # i, and I denotes the unit matrix.

A.6 Transformation of cylindrical waves into space harmonics

Using Equation (A.55) and (A.56) in equation (A.8) the scattered field at an arbitrary point in the rectangular waveguide can be accurately calculated in terms of the multi-pole fields. However it is more useful for practical applications to obtain the solutions in terms of the model fields of the waveguide. For this purpose the multi-pole fields are transformed into a series of mode fields using the following formulae.

$$
\sum_{l=-\infty}^{\infty} H_m^{(1)}(k\rho_{i,l})e^{im\phi_{i,l}} = \frac{2(-i)^m}{hk^m} \sum_{v=-\infty}^{\infty} \frac{(k_{x,v} - ik_{z,v})^m}{k_{z,v}} e^{-ik_{x,v}\Delta_i} e^{i(k_{x,v}x - k_{z,v}z)} \quad \text{(For } z \le -d_i)
\tag{A.66}
$$

$$
\sum_{l=-\infty}^{\infty} H_m^{(1)}(k\rho_{i,l})e^{im\phi_{i,l}} = \frac{2(-i)^m}{hk^m} \sum_{v=-\infty}^{\infty} \frac{(k_{x,v} + ik_{z,v})^m}{k_{z,v}} e^{-ik_{x,v}\Delta_i} e^{i(k_{x,v}x + k_{z,v}z)} \quad \text{(For } z \ge d_i)
$$

$$\tag{A.67}$$

$$\sum_{l=-\infty}^{\infty} H_m^{(1)}(k\rho'_{i,l})e^{-im\phi'_{i,l}} = \frac{2(i)^m}{hk^m} \sum_{v=-\infty}^{\infty} \frac{(k_{x,v}+ik_{z,v})^m}{k_{z,v}} e^{ik_{x,v}\Delta_i} e^{i(k_{x,v}x-k_{z,v}z)} \quad \text{(For } z \le -d_i\text{)}$$

$$\tag{A.68}$$

$$\sum_{l=-\infty}^{\infty} H_m^{(1)}(k\rho'_{i,l})e^{-im\phi'_{i,l}} = \frac{2(i)^m}{hk^m} \sum_{v=-\infty}^{\infty} \frac{(k_{x,v}-ik_{z,v})^m}{k_{z,v}} e^{ik_{x,v}\Delta_i} e^{i(k_{x,v}x+k_{z,v}z)} \quad \text{(For } z \ge d_i\text{)}$$

These formulae can be deduced from the recurrence formula for Hankel functions $H_m^{(1)}(k_0\rho_{i,l})e^{im\phi_{i,l}}$ and Fourier integral representation for the zero-order Hankel function $H_0^{(1)}(k_0\rho_{i,l})$. Using equation (A.66) – (A.69) in Equation (A.8), the scattered fields in $z \le -\sup(r_1, r_2)$ and in $z \ge \sup(r_1, r_2)$ which indicate the reflected fields and transmitted field, respectively are given below.

A.7 Expressions for Reflected and Transmitted Fields

$$E_y^r = \sum_{l=-\infty}^{\infty} \sum_{m=-\infty}^{\infty} X_{1,m} [H_m^{(1)}(k\rho_{1,l})e^{im\phi_{1,l}} - (-1)^m H_m^{(1)}(k\rho'_{1,l})e^{-im\phi'_{1,l}}]$$

$$+ \sum_{l=-\infty}^{\infty} \sum_{m=-\infty}^{\infty} X_{2,m} [H_m^{(1)}(k\rho_{2,l})e^{im\phi_{2,l}} - (-1)^m H_m^{(1)}(k\rho'_{2,l})e^{-im\phi'_{2,l}}] \tag{A.70}$$

$$= \sum_{v=-\infty}^{\infty} (\mathbf{u}_{1,v}^+ + \mathbf{u}_{1,v}^-) \cdot \mathbf{X}_1 \sin(k_{x,v}x)e^{-ik_{z,v}z} + \sum_{v=-\infty}^{\infty} (\mathbf{u}_{2,v}^+ + \mathbf{u}_{2,v}^-) \cdot \mathbf{X}_2 \sin(k_{x,v}x)e^{-ik_{z,v}z}$$

$$E_y^t = \sum_{l=-\infty}^{\infty} \sum_{m=-\infty}^{\infty} X_{1,m} [H_m^{(1)}(k\rho_{1,l})e^{im\phi_{1,l}} - (-1)^m H_m^{(1)}(k\rho'_{1,l})e^{-im\phi'_{1,l}}]$$

$$+ \sum_{l=-\infty}^{\infty} \sum_{m=-\infty}^{\infty} X_{2,m} [H_m^{(1)}(k\rho_{2,l})e^{im\phi_{2,l}} - (-1)^m H_m^{(1)}(k\rho'_{2,l})e^{-im\phi'_{2,l}}]$$

$$+ a_\mu^+ \sin(k_{x,\mu}x)e^{ik_{z,\mu}z} \tag{A.71}$$

$$= \sum_{v=-\infty}^{\infty} (\mathbf{v}_{1,v}^+ + \mathbf{v}_{1,v}^-) \cdot \mathbf{X}_1 \sin(k_{x,v}x)e^{ik_{z,v}z} + \sum_{v=-\infty}^{\infty} (\mathbf{v}_{2,v}^+ + \mathbf{v}_{2,v}^-) \cdot \mathbf{X}_2 \sin(k_{x,v}x)e^{ik_{z,v}z}$$

$$+ a_\mu^+ \sin(k_{x,\mu}x)e^{ik_{z,\mu}z}$$

$$\mathbf{u}_{i,v}^\pm = [u_{i,vm}^\pm] = \left[\frac{2(\pm i)^{m-1}}{ak_{z,v}} \frac{(k_{x,v} \pm ik_{z,v})^m}{k^m} e^{\pm ik_{x,v}\Delta_i} \right] \tag{A.72}$$

$$\mathbf{v}_{i,v}^\pm = [v_{i,vm}^\pm] = \left[\frac{2(\pm i)^{m-1}}{ak_{z,v}} \frac{(k_{x,v} \mp ik_{z,v})^m}{k^m} e^{\pm ik_{x,v}\Delta_i} \right] \tag{A.73}$$

A.8 Reflection and Transmission Coefficients

Substituting Equation (A.55) and (A.56) into Equation (A.70) and (A.71), the reflected and transmitted fields are expressed as

$$
\left(
\begin{aligned}
E_y^r &= \sum_{v=-\infty}^{\infty} (\mathbf{u}_{1,v}^+ + \mathbf{u}_{1,v}^-) \cdot (\mathbf{S}_{11} \cdot \mathbf{p}_{1,\mu}^+ + \mathbf{S}_{12} \cdot \mathbf{p}_{2,\mu}^+) a_\mu^+ \sin(k_{x,v} x) e^{-ik_{z,v} z} \\
&\quad + \sum_{v=-\infty}^{\infty} (\mathbf{u}_{2,v}^+ + \mathbf{u}_{2,v}^-) \cdot (\mathbf{S}_{21} \cdot \mathbf{p}_{1,\mu}^+ + \mathbf{S}_{22} \cdot \mathbf{p}_{2,\mu}^+) a_\mu^+ \sin(k_{x,v} x) e^{-ik_{z,v} z} \\
E_y^t &= \sum_{v=-\infty}^{\infty} (\mathbf{v}_{1,v}^+ + \mathbf{v}_{1,v}^-) \cdot (\mathbf{S}_{11} \cdot \mathbf{p}_{1,\mu}^+ + \mathbf{S}_{12} \cdot \mathbf{p}_{2,\mu}^+) a_\mu^+ \sin(k_{x,v} x) e^{ik_{z,v} z} \\
&\quad + \sum_{v=-\infty}^{\infty} (\mathbf{v}_{2,v}^+ + \mathbf{v}_{2,v}^-) \cdot (\mathbf{S}_{21} \cdot \mathbf{p}_{1,\mu}^+ + \mathbf{S}_{22} \cdot \mathbf{p}_{2,\mu}^+) a_\mu^+ \sin(k_{x,v} x) e^{ik_{z,v} z} \\
&\quad + a_\mu^+ \sin(k_{x,\mu} x) e^{ik_{z,\mu} z}
\end{aligned}
\right)
\tag{A.74}
$$

From Equation (A.74) reflection coefficient $r^-{}_{v\mu}$ is defined as $\mathbf{r}^- = [r_v^-]$ and the transmission coefficient $f_{v\mu}^-$ as $\mathbf{f}^+ = [f_v^+]$ into TE_{v0} mode for the incidence of the forward propagating $TE_{\mu 0}$ mode with following form,

$$
E_y^r = \sum_{v=-\infty}^{\infty} a_v^- \sin(k_{x,v} x) e^{-ik_{z,v} z} = \sum_{v=-\infty}^{\infty} a_\mu^+ r_v^- \sin(k_{x,v} x) e^{-ik_{z,v} z}
\tag{A.75}
$$

$$
E_y^t = \sum_{v=-\infty}^{\infty} a_v^+ \sin(k_{x,v} x) e^{ik_{z,v} z} = \sum_{v=-\infty}^{\infty} a_\mu^+ f_v^+ \sin(k_{x,v} x) e^{ik_{z,v} z}
\tag{A.76}
$$

$$
\begin{aligned}
\mathbf{r}^- &= \mathbf{U}_1 \cdot (\mathbf{S}_{11} \cdot \mathbf{p}_{1,\mu}^+ + \mathbf{S}_{12} \cdot \mathbf{p}_{2,\mu}^+) + \mathbf{U}_2 \cdot (\mathbf{S}_{21} \cdot \mathbf{p}_{1,\mu}^+ + \mathbf{S}_{22} \cdot \mathbf{p}_{2,\mu}^+) \\
&= (\mathbf{U}_1 \mathbf{S}_{11} + \mathbf{U}_2 \mathbf{S}_{21}) \cdot \mathbf{p}_{1,\mu}^+ + (\mathbf{U}_1 \mathbf{S}_{12} + \mathbf{U}_2 \mathbf{S}_{22}) \cdot \mathbf{p}_{2,\mu}^+
\end{aligned}
\tag{A.77}
$$

$$
\mathbf{f}^+ = \delta_{v\mu} + (\mathbf{V}_1 \mathbf{S}_{11} + \mathbf{V}_2 \mathbf{S}_{21}) \cdot \mathbf{p}_{1,\mu}^+ + (\mathbf{V}_1 \mathbf{S}_{12} + \mathbf{V}_2 \mathbf{S}_{22}) \cdot \mathbf{p}_{2,\mu}^+ \qquad \text{where}
\tag{A.78}
$$

$$
\mathbf{r}^- = [r_v^-]
\tag{AI.79}
$$

$$
\mathbf{f}^+ = [f_v^+]
\tag{A.80}
$$

$$
\mathbf{U}_i = [u_{i,vm}] = [u_{i,vm}^+ + u_{i,vm}^-] \quad (i=1,2)
\tag{A.81}
$$

$$
\mathbf{V_i} = [v_{i,vm}] = [v_{i,vm}^+ + v_{i,vm}^-]
\tag{A.82}
$$

The last term in Equation (A.71) represents the incident field defined by Equation (A.1).

A.9 2D T-Matrix of a circular cylinder

The T-matrix T_i ($i = 1, 2$) plays important role in the present formulation. It describes the detail of scattering of T_E wave from each post element in isolation. Any analytical or numerical technique can be employed to calculate the T- matrix. If the vertical cylindrical post has a circular cross section with a radius r, the T-matrix becomes a diagonal matrix and it can be obtained in closed form for various configurations of post material as dielectric or perfect conducting.

The T-matrix can be obtained in closed form especially when the cylindrical object has a circular cross section. For a circular dielectric cylinder with radius r, permittivity ε and permeability μ, the following relations are used for theoretical computation for elements of T- matrix. The expression for τ_m for two typical configurations can be derived and written as follows.

$$T = [\tau_m \delta_{mm'}]$$ (A.83)

(a) Circular post of dielectric with permittivity ε and permeability μ with

$$\tau_m = \frac{\zeta_0 J_m(k_0 r) J_m'(kr) - \zeta J_m(kr) J_m'(k_0 r)}{\zeta_0 J_m(kr) H_m^{(1)}(k_0 r) - \zeta J_m(kr) H_m^{'(1)}(k_0 r)} \quad \text{TM wave}$$ (A.84)

$$= -\frac{\zeta J_m(k_0 r) - \tau_0 J_m(kr) J_m'(k_0 r)}{\zeta J_m'(kr) H_m^{(1)}(k_0 r) - \zeta_0 J_m(kr) H_m^{'(1)}(k_0 r)} \quad \text{TE wave}$$ (A.85)

with $\zeta_0 = \sqrt{\dfrac{\mu_0}{\varepsilon_0}}$ and $\zeta = \sqrt{\dfrac{\mu}{\varepsilon}}$

(b) Circular post of perfect electric conductor

$$\tau_m = \frac{J_m(k_0 r)}{H_m^{(1)}(k_0 r)} \quad \text{(TM wave)}$$ (A.86)

$$\tau_m = -\frac{J_m'(k_0 r)}{H_m^{'(1)}(k_0 r)} \quad \text{(TE wave)}$$ (A.87)

where J_m' and $H_m^{'(1)}$ denote the derivative with respect to the indicated arguments and $\delta_{mm'}$ is the Kronekar delta. The solutions to the scattering problem of a single layer of two posts are completed by Equations (A.75) and (A.76) or Equation (A.77) or (A.78). Here the reflection and transmission coefficient as given by Equation (A.77) and (A.78) is derived from the reflection and transmission matrices for the two posts and is used for further calculation process of eight layer two post problem.

Again for the N stacked structure, reflection and transmission matrices R_j^{+-}, F_j^{+-} for each post are successfully concatenated over the number of posts to obtain generalized reflection and transmission matrices for the entire system.

AI.10 Algorithm to find out reflection coefficient and transmission coefficient of multi-post multi-layered waveguide filter

1. Declaration of normalized parameters (frequency band , waveguide dimension, post dimension and dielectric constant , interlayer gap , inter-post separation)
2. Calculation of propagation constant
3. Set up matrix elements for y component of incident E Field as per Equation (A.1-A.7)
4. Set up matrix elements for scattered E field as per Equation (A.8-A.10)
5. Calculation of Roots of Bessel function and Hankel function
6. Calculation of Lattice Sum according to Equation (A.35-A.40)
7. Calculation of T matrix as per Equation (A.83-A.87)
8. Calculation of total field for forward propagating wave and the same for backward propagating wave as per Equation (A.41) and (A.53) respectively.
9. Calculation of boundary conditions for the forward scattered field and backward scattered fields according to Equation (A.41) and (A.53)
10. The unknown amplitude vectors as per Equation (A.42) and (A.54) are calculated in terms of T matrix and Lattice Sum using the expressions (A.55) - (A.60)
11. Scattering parameters are directly related with unknown amplitude vectors and as per Equations (A.64) and (A.65) which can be calculated by solving Equations (A.62) and (A.63)
12. In terms of modal fields the scattering reflectance and transmittance are calculated using Equation (A.66) –(A.69)
13. Substituting equation (A.55) and (A.56) into Equation (A.70) and (A.71), the reflected and transmitted fields are calculated from Equation (A.74)
14. Reflection and Transmission coefficient as given by equation (A.77) and (A.78) is derived from the reflection and transmission matrices
15. The reflection coefficients and transmission coefficients are calculated from Equation (A.73) - (A.82) for the single layer two posts inside rectangular waveguide and are used for further calculation process of eight layer two post problem
16. For the N stacked structure, reflection and transmission matrices R_j^{+-}, F_j^{+-} for each post are successfully concatenated over the number of posts to obtain generalized reflection and transmission matrices for the entire system

17. Finally within a frequency band the reflection coefficient and transmission coefficients are calculated for a waveguide structure having single layer two posts using a iterative loop. The data generated is stored and used for further calculation

18. The frequency response of S-parameters of waveguide structure having multi-layered dielectric posts is also generated using this data

19. The data file is used for testing and training of ANN model for few waveguide filter having multiple dielectric posts in multi-layered configuration

20. The performance of trained ANN model over a specified frequency range is evaluated in terms of standard error and further verification by EM simulation is done to compare the design, simulation and measured results

MATLAB code is developed using the algorithm and used for GA optimization. The first few lines of the code set the parameters of GA uses (i) number and length of the chromosomes, (ii) crossover and mutation rates and (iii) number of generations in binary representation scheme. An initial uniformly distributed random binary population is created. The objective function is then evaluated to produce the vector of objective values. In the generational loop a fitness vector is determined and selected individuals are recombined using single-point crossover applied with probability = 0.7. Binary mutation is then applied to the offspring with probability = 0.0175 and the objective function values for the new individuals are calculated. Finally the new individuals are re-inserted in the population and the generation counter is incremented. The GA terminates after maximum iterations set by the generational loop.

CPSIA information can be obtained
at www.ICGtesting.com
Printed in the USA
LVHW080525101222
734929LV00013B/571